The Evil That Surrounds Us

The Evil
That Surrounds Us

THE WWII MEMOIR OF ERNA BECKER-KOHEN

EDITED AND TRANSLATED BY
KEVIN P. SPICER AND MARTINA CUCCHIARA

INDIANA UNIVERSITY PRESS

This book is a publication of

INDIANA UNIVERSITY PRESS
Office of Scholarly Publishing
Herman B Wells Library 350
1320 East 10th Street
Bloomington, Indiana 47405 USA

iupress.indiana.edu

© 2017 by Esther-Maria Nägele

*Manufactured in the
United States of America*

Library of Congress
Cataloging-in-Publication Data

Names: Becker-Kohen, Erna, 1906-1987, author. | Spicer, Kevin P., 1965– editor, translator. | Cucchiara, Martina, editor, translator.
Title: The evil that surrounds us : the WWII memoir of Erna Becker-Kohen / edited and translated by Kevin P. Spicer and Martina Cucchiara.
Description: Bloomington : Indiana University Press, [2017]
Identifiers: LCCN 2017029275 (print) | LCCN 2017035159 (ebook) | ISBN 9780253029904 (e-book) | ISBN 9780253029577 (cloth : alk. paper) | ISBN 9780253029867 (pbk. : alk. paper)
Subjects: LCSH: Becker-Kohen, Erna, 1906-1987. | Jews—Germany—History—1933-1945—Biography. | Holocaust, Jewish (1939-1945)—Germany—Personal narratives. | World War, 1939-1945—Personal narratives, Jewish. | Jews—Germany—Diaries. | Germany—Biography.
Classification: LCC DS134.42.B424 (ebook) | LCC DS134.42.B424 A3 2017 (print) | DDC 940.53/18092 [B] —dc23
LC record available at https://lccn.loc.gov /2017029275

1 2 3 4 5 22 21 20 19 18 17

Contents

Acknowledgments

WE WOULD LIKE TO THANK THE MANY INDIVIDUALS AND IN-stitutions that have assisted us in the compilation of the memoir of Erna Becker-Kohen. First and foremost, we are grateful to Erna's granddaughter, Esther-Maria Nägele, and her husband, Matthias Nägele, for trusting us with this project and for their tireless assistance as we completed the work. We thank Dee Mortensen and Robert Sloan, our editors at Indiana University Press, as well as our anonymous readers for their kind and constructive feedback. Ilse Andrews and James William Chichetto, C.S.C., offered helpful suggestions on style and prose. Bluff-ton University Research Center and the Office of Academic Affairs of Stonehill College provided valuable financial support. We are also in-debted to the many archivists, scholars, librarians, and local historians who have responded to our numerous inquiries, especially Anne Alsheimer, Elizabeth Anthony, Timothy V. Bender, Berta Birzele, Rudolf Brodkborb, Suzanne Brown-Fleming, Ron Coleman, Michael Cucchi-ara, Martin Dean, Michael Fliri, Amy Houston, Mary Jean Johnson, Martin Kapferer, Susanne Kaup, Gotthard Klein, Brigitte Klöpf, Sabine Kröß-Tunner, Susanne Lamsouguer, Kassian Lauterer, O.Cist., Angela Martin, Jürgen Matthäus, Frank Mecklenburg, Johannes Mertens,

Thomas Mitterecker, Lukas Morscher, Erwin Naimer, Audra Oglesbee, Heather Perry, Bertold Pölcher, Katharina Rumpf, Brigitte Schneider, Vincent Slatt, Kathrin Tannheimer, Martina Wagner, Andrea Widauer, Jürgen Wolf, and Hildegard Zellinger-Kratzl.

The Evil That Surrounds Us

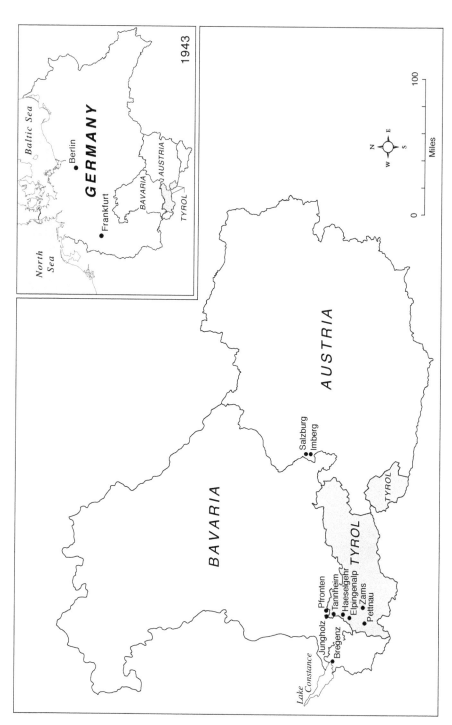

Locations of Erna and Silvan Becker's flight in the 1940s. Map created by Barry Levely.

Introduction

ON JULY 3, 1931, GUSTAV BECKER AND ERNA KOHEN MARRIED. Gustav was thirty, Erna twenty-five. Photographs of Erna from the 1920s depict a vivacious young woman whose pretty face showed no trace of the strain and solemnity that marked her features in later years. But even then, all was not well. Gustav and Erna married during the Great Depression, and we do not know if the economic misery and political instability that was menacing Germany at the time was already casting a shadow over the couple's happiness. Perhaps Gustav and Erna resolutely banished all gloomy thoughts that day, secure in the knowledge that they were more fortunate than many, since earlier that year Gustav had found work as an engineer with the radio manufacturer Reinhardt & Co. in Berlin. The newlyweds settled into comfortable bourgeois surroundings in Berlin-Treptow.

The Beckers were new to Berlin. Born in 1901, Gustav hailed from a Catholic family of civil servants in the medium-sized city of Darmstadt in southwestern Germany, where he had also completed his university studies in engineering. Erna was born in 1906 in Cologne. She was the third of five children of assimilated Jewish parents whose families had lived in Germany for generations.[1] When Erna was four years old, her father, Heinrich Kohen, moved his wife and children to Frankfurt am

Main. He died soon thereafter, when Erna was only ten years old. But even in reduced circumstances, her mother, Isabella Kohen, made sure that her children received an excellent education. Erna and Gustav were thus evenly matched in class and education. According to Erna, the fact that she was Jewish and Gustav Roman Catholic posed no obstacle to their courtship and marriage.[2] In 1931, Erna and Gustav could not have known that their religious affiliations, which had mattered so little to them during their courtship, would define their marriage under Nazism.

On January 30, 1933, Adolf Hitler became chancellor of Germany. As a Jew, Erna became an outcast overnight. As her husband, Gustav shared in Erna's bewildering experience of violence, fear, and social isolation, which engulfed Germany's Jews after January 1933.

Gustav's status as an "Aryan" decisively shaped Erna's experience of persecution in Nazi Germany. In 1939, Erna was one of 20,454 Jews in Germany married to an Aryan (non-Jewish German) spouse.[3] Erna and Gustav's "mixed marriage" was "privileged," which meant that on account of her non-Jewish husband, Erna was exempt from the most radical anti-Jewish measures.[4] As of December 1938, the Nazi regime considered marriages between non-Jewish and Jewish German men and women privileged, provided couples did not raise their children in the Jewish faith. A childless mixed marriage was privileged only if the wife was Jewish and the husband Aryan. Hence, a childless marriage between a Jewish German man and a non-Jewish German woman was "nonprivileged." A marriage was also considered nonprivileged if the Aryan partner, usually the wife, had converted to Judaism or, as alluded to above, if the couple raised their children in the Jewish faith.[5] Although Erna's marriage was privileged, her harrowing narrative of isolation, flight, and persecution shatters any notion of favorable treatment that the term implies.[6]

The very poignancy and persuasiveness of the author's writing raise important questions about the text's creation and genre. The manuscript Erna deposited with the Leo Baeck Institute in 1976 resembles a diary in that it consists of a series of dated entries that begin in 1937 and end in 1963.[7] But the form of a diary is less important than the time of its creation. Inherent in the term "diary" is the expectation that the text was produced close to the day-by-day events it describes. A diarist is ignorant

Erna Kohen as a young woman.
Courtesy of Esther-Maria Nägele.

Erna and Gustav Becker on their
wedding day in 1931. Courtesy of
Esther-Maria Nägele.

of the future, and her writings reflect a "gradual acquisition of knowledge and shifting values that occur in life."[8] Although "all telling modifies what is being told," the diarist's close proximity to events renders her account more authentic in most historians' eyes.[9]

Holocaust memoirs, written months or years after the events in question took place, are more problematic for some scholars. There is the concern that the passage of time, coupled with the frailty of the author's memory, cannot but alter the past. Authors of memoirs further complicate the historian's task by usurping it through the imposition of "certain literary conventions" onto the text, such as chronology, a story line, and a narrative voice.[10] Readers of Erna's writings will quickly discern that the text's neat time line and story arc, roughly bracketed by the birth of her son Silvan in 1938 and the death of Gustav in 1952, resemble the literary format of a memoir, albeit presented in the form of a diary.

At the same time, the author's emotionally raw voice seems genuine and close at hand to her circumstances. This may be because Erna wrote her narrative in the immediate postwar period in Bregenz, Austria.[11] Perhaps she adopted the format of a diary because in writing her memoir, she did not rely just on her memory but used notes she kept "on the spot" throughout her ordeal.[12] The first definitive record of the memoir's existence may be found in a November 18, 1958, article in the *Badische Zeitung*. The article reports that Erna gave a public reading from the memoir to members and guests of the Catholic German Women's League in Freiburg im Breisgau.[13]

Numerous scholars have utilized Erna's memoir in their work on Jews in Nazi Germany.[14] The editors' research of persons, places, and events, discussed in the narrative and presented in extensive annotations, further strengthens the text's historic value. At the same time, Erna did not write as an impartial historian whose sole objective was to relay a series of historical events. Rather, as a survivor, Erna claimed the authority of what one scholar called a "moral witness," a writer on a "testimonial mission with a moral purpose."[15] In this role, Erna strove for a truthful portrayal of her experiences under National Socialism without seeking to remain neutral. In particular, Erna interpreted her experience of persecution through the lens of Christianity. Thus, at least in part, her narrative constitutes a deliberate reckoning, a stinging indictment of a Christian people, who, full of hatred and malice toward Jews, nonetheless claimed as their central tenet "love of neighbor."

Shunned and despised by her Christian neighbors, Erna still sought answers and community in the Christian faith. When her fear of what was yet to come threatened to overwhelm her, she sought out a Jesuit priest who listened to her with empathy and kindness. As she received instruction in the Catholic faith, Erna "saw a light and yearned to be one of them."[16] She converted to Roman Catholicism in 1936.[17]

Erna's mother, Isabella Kohen, saw her daughter's baptism as a paradox and betrayal. She accused her daughter of having "joined her enemies." Erna herself remained deeply conflicted about her conversion, which was, at least partially, the consequence of persecution and exclusion. Readers become privy to the intense struggles she fought within herself over her decision to become a Catholic. She was often tormented by doubts, especially when the persecution of Jews worsened. At the same time, she insisted that "true Christians" were not her enemies and she relentlessly searched for them, first out of a desire for community and acceptance and later out of a desperate need for assistance. Erna's memoir is therefore also a memorial to these true Christians, Father Erwin Röhr, Maria Herberg, Binosa Zobl, Michl Lochbihler, and others, who stood by her when almost everyone else had deserted her. By not abandoning a Jew in Nazi Germany, these individuals refused to act out a core tenet of Nazi ideology: the rejection and exclusion of Jews, which became key prerequisites for their eventual murder in the Holocaust.

JEWISH PERSECUTION IN NAZI GERMANY

Hitler blamed Jews for the widespread despair brought on by economic depression and the humiliation of a lost war. He also promised redemption and restoration of national greatness through the ruthless practice of racial hygiene, the merciless persecution and complete exclusion of people considered a threat to the racial purity of the *Volksgemeinschaft* (people's racial community).[18]

Starting in 1933, the regime promulgated numerous laws and decrees with the explicit aim of excluding Jews from the German economy. The first major anti-Jewish legislation, the Law for the Restoration of the Professional Civil Service of April 11, 1933, decreed the dismissal of Jews from civil service positions with only certain limited exceptions.[19] It defined as non-Aryan anyone descended from at least one non-Aryan, chiefly Jewish parent or grandparent.[20] Since the Nazis' definition of Jewishness relied, in part, on the religion of Germans' ancestors, Erna remained racially Jewish under Nazi law, even after her conversion to Catholicism. She also remained subject to all anti-Jewish decrees because, as stated previously, until 1938, the Nazis afforded no special treatment to Jews married to Aryans.[21] Erna was nonetheless spared the National Socialist regime's immediate and widening economic assault on Jews since her Aryan husband's position as an engineer was not yet threatened by his mixed marriage.

Gustav could shield Erna from economic ruin but not from the maliciousness of their neighbors. Erna's testimony illuminates the extent to which the Nazi regime depended on ordinary Germans to participate in the persecution of Jews by acting out and enforcing its antisemitic ideology and decrees in daily life. In particular, after the proclamation of the Nuremberg Laws in September 1935, which forbade marriages and intimate relationships between Jews and non-Jews, Nazi anti-Jewish measures reached deep into Germans' private spheres.[22] Enforcement of these measures thus depended on the vigilance of Jews' neighbors, acquaintances, and coworkers.[23]

Aryan Germans were vital in helping to create the climate of unabated fear and terror that became the grim reality for Jews across Germany. Jews could not feel safe anytime or anywhere, least of all in their homes and neighborhoods. Erna dreaded her neighbors in Berlin. By 1940, Erna and Gustav's social isolation was absolute. No one except the Catholic priest, Father Erwin Röhr, dared to set foot in the Beckers' apartment. When a well-meaning neighbor tried to befriend Erna in August 1941, vigilant observers immediately threatened to report the neighbor to the Gestapo; she never spoke to Erna again.[24]

Erna's own terror of the Gestapo was well founded. In Nazi Germany, Jews confronted the absurd situation of ever more oppressive laws that curtailed their lives alongside increasing lawlessness in the form of violent physical and verbal assaults. Moreover, if they became victims of crimes, Jews could no longer count on police protection.[25] Thus, it is not surprising that on the eve of the Second World War, Gustav feared that "people in their war euphoria" could beat his Jewish wife and son to death. But despite the worsening persecution the Beckers experienced after the start of the conflict on September 1, 1939, on account of her privileged status, Erna was exempt from the deportation of Jews that commenced in the fall of 1941.

Hitler had created the designation of privileged marriage in December 1938, in the wake of the *Kristallnacht* pogrom (November 9–10), which marked a key escalation of the persecution of Jews. During that night, Storm Troopers (SA) and Hitler Youth members and ordinary Germans destroyed German Jewish homes, businesses, and synagogues while also murdering approximately ninety-one Jews and injuring hundreds more.[26] Between November 1938 and September 1939, the Nazi government also issued 229 additional anti-Jewish decrees that whittled away at the few remaining freedoms that existed for Jews.[27]

The question arises: Why did Hitler create the category of privileged marriage in 1938, even though he believed that intermarried Jews posed a particular danger to the people's community? In his manifesto, *Mein Kampf*, Hitler purported that the racially superior Northern European Aryan had to be protected from inferior races. Any "racial crossing," he believed, was dangerous because "Historical experience . . . shows with terrifying clarity that in every mingling of Aryan blood with that of lower peoples the result was the end of the cultured people."[28] This ideology became law in September 1935 through the above-mentioned Nuremberg Laws that forbade sexual relations and future marriages between Jews and non-Jews. But Hitler nonetheless refused to side with hard-liners in the National Socialist Workers' Party and the German government, who repeatedly pressed him not just to prohibit future mixed marriages but also to dissolve existing unions between Jews and non-Jews by fiat.[29]

One of these hard-liners was the Security Squad (Schutzstaffel), or SS, general Reinhard Heydrich. At the Wannsee Conference in January 1942, where Heydrich convened Nazi functionaries to coordinate the murder of European Jews, he demanded the inclusion of intermarried Jews and persons of mixed blood in the Final Solution. In response, Wilhelm Stuckart, a lawyer and secretary of state in the Ministry of the Interior, suggested that the state simply dissolve mixed marriages by decree.[30] However, at a subsequent meeting in March 1942, representatives of the propaganda ministry rejected Stuckart's proposal out of concerns over the certain and unpredictable interventions on the part of the churches.[31]

The churches had a particular interest in the issue. A sizable number of Germans in mixed marriages were considered Jewish under Nazi racial laws but, like Erna, were in fact Christians.[32] Most likely the threat of the Catholic Church's public intervention in the matter, along with the regime's unwillingness to alienate the Aryan relatives of intermarried Jews, stayed Hitler's hand.[33] Nazi officials continued to debate the issue of compulsory divorce but it was never settled because Hitler refused to make a decision on the matter.[34]

ERNA BECKER-KOHEN'S FAMILY AND EMIGRATION

Keenly aware of her privileged status, Erna wrote in April 1939, "I am safe after all on account of [Gustav's] Aryan ancestry." Erna's privilege, however, did not include her extended family. In her memoir, Erna does not just recount her own story. She also illuminates the myriad ways the Nazis shattered and destroyed her family. She describes how her mother, Isabella Kohen, was "driven from her home" in April 1939 and given "a shabby room." The loss of her home was the result of governmental practices imposed regionally in 1937 and mandated throughout the Reich in April 1939. This specific operation, codified into the Law concerning Tenancy Contracts with Jews, compelled Jews to relocate to designated buildings, identified as "Jew Houses" (*Judenhäuser*). Unlike the ghettos established during the Second World War in occupied territories, the *Judenhäuser* were not isolated to a particular section of any given city or town.[35]

The April 1939 law is but one example of the sharp increase in state discriminatory measures against Jews following *Kristallnacht*. The sheer volume of these anti-Jewish decrees, coupled with the violence of the event itself, convinced many more German and Austrian Jews to make plans to leave Germany.[36] However, emigration was easier said than done. In July 1938, months before *Kristallnacht*, delegates from thirty-two countries had gathered at the French resort town of Evian-les-Bains to discuss the impending refugee crisis. Before the conference's conclusion, it became imminently clear that no country, with the exception of the Dominican Republic, was willing to raise its existing quota to allow more Jewish immigration. Even the Dominican Republic's openness was self-serving, meant only to benefit the country financially through the immigration of "wealthy" Jews, and to repair its international reputation after its recently committed atrocities against guest Haitian workers.[37] Thus, there were few places for German and Austrian Jews to seek refuge. Similarly, the Nazi government made it incredibly daunting for Jews to emigrate, by requiring an "enormous mass of paperwork" and charging various fees and taxes before anyone could be cleared to leave.[38]

It was all the more fortunate for Erna's sister, Ruth Seegmüller, and her husband, in May 1939, to receive a visa and immigrate to Chile, a country that gave refuge to approximately 12,000 Jews from 1933 to 1941.[39] Ruth and her husband were able to take advantage of a narrow window of opportunity provided by the 1938 election of Pedro Aguirre Cerda as president of Chile. Aguirre Cerda reversed the anti-immigration stance of his predecessor and promised that his country would provide a refuge for anyone seeking asylum. Although Aguirre Cerda's government endeavored to fulfill this promise, corruption and antisemitism among Chilean consul personnel ensured that many Jews were denied visas.[40]

Between 1933 and the outbreak of war between Germany and Poland on September 1, 1939, approximately 282,000 Jews emigrated from Germany and 117,000 from Austria.[41] In the interim years until October 23, 1941, when Heinrich Himmler, the head of the SS, ordered an end to Jewish emigration from the German Reich,[42] an additional 71,500 Jews left Germany.[43] Still, the outbreak of war made emigration much harder, as Erna attests in her diary entry of August 1940, which describes the plight of her mother, Isabella, who, despite purchasing a ticket and procuring a visa, was still unable to join her daughter, Ruth, in Chile.[44] In a later entry, dated April 1943, Erna states that her mother died a natural death in Brussels, where she had been living since the summer of 1940. She attributed this death to the stress brought on by the arrest of her brother, Max Kohen, that same summer.

CONCENTRATION AND DEATH CAMPS

In her March 1941 diary entry, Erna laments the internment of her brother Max in a concentration camp in the Eastern Pyrenees region of

France. Prior to this time, Max, like Erna's mother, Isabella, had been living in Belgium as a refugee from Nazi persecution.[45] On May 10, 1940, when the German Wehrmacht (the unified armed forces of Nazi Germany) invaded Belgium, Belgian authorities negated their promises to provide shelter for refugees from Nazi Germany, most of whom were Jewish, and ordered males who possessed German passports to report at once to the Belgian police. Those who did not follow instructions were subject to arrest. Within days, Belgian authorities deported the majority of the rounded-up refugees in boxcars to France following an agreement between the governments of these two countries.[46] Max was among the deportees while his mother, Isabella, his wife, Martha, and their son, Heinz, remained in Belgium, which soon unconditionally surrendered to Germany. On the same day that the German Wehrmacht invaded Belgium, German troops also launched a blitzkrieg attack on France. As bombs fell, French authorities routed the train carrying Max and his fellow refugees through the French countryside to the final destination of Saint-Cyprien, a town on the southern coast near France's border with Spain.[47] In this idyllic coastal town, the remains of a camp, originally established to house refugees from the Spanish Civil War, lay partially intact. The camp's original perimeters were now demarcated with rows upon rows of razor-sharp barbed wire. It was now a verifiable prison and everything about it was primitive in nature. The internees, for example, slept on a thin layer of straw covering the sandy beachfront earth on which the entire camp sat.[48] Soon, dysentery, typhoid, and even malaria were serious concerns for all confined there.[49]

By mid-June, French officials acknowledged defeat and signed an armistice with Germany, which divided the country into two regions, the north and west occupied by Germany and the south administrated from the city of Vichy by an authoritative government composed of appeasing French officials. Saint-Cyprien was located within a region under the authority of Vichy administrators, though German authorities made it clear that whenever they wished they could demand the handover of any of the internees.[50] Despite this looming threat, the situation temporarily spared the internees from falling into German hands. Less than five months later, the landscape changed after a storm led to severe flooding of the camp, leading French authorities to close it in late October 1940.

On October 29, Max was transferred to Gurs internment camp in south-western France near the border between Vichy and occupied France.[51] He remained there until June 27, 1941, when he was moved to Noé, pri-marily a "hospital camp," directly east of Gurs.[52] The reason for Max's transfer is unclear; however, it is possible that he was sent there for medi-cal treatment. At some point, Max was transferred again, this time to Septfonds internment camp, just north of Noé. In August 1942, the Vichy administration turned Max and thousands of German Jewish refugees over to the SS who, in turn, placed them temporarily in Drancy transit camp located just outside of Paris.[53] On August 28, 1942, Max was deported from Drancy to Auschwitz on the twenty-fifth transport.[54] Erna does not record learning of her brother's fate until her October 1945 entry. There is no specific record of when Max perished in Auschwitz.

Erna lost the majority of her siblings and extended family during the Holocaust. Some, like Max, lost their lives in Auschwitz, which together with Majdanek, served a twofold function—as a death camp and slave labor camp—though the harshness of the latter coupled with malnutri-tion and disease regularly resulted in death for camp prisoners. Other camps, such as Sobibor, Treblinka, and Bełżec, served only as places of destruction where Jews were murdered immediately on arrival. The only Jews kept alive in these camps were those who belonged to the *Sonderkom-mando* (special units), whom the SS forced into slavery to facilitate the killing process. These death camps and slave labor camps were located on occupied Polish soil and constructed after the Second World War had begun.[55]

Prior to the outbreak of war, the SS had established an elaborate series of camps throughout Germany that grew in number as the country ex-tended its borders. From the moment Hitler entered office as chancellor of Germany in late January 1933, some form of detention or concentra-tion camp, distinct from the country's traditional penal system, existed. At first, such detention camps sprang up in seemingly haphazard fashion in abandoned factories, empty buildings, and other similar structures as SA and SS men initially "dealt" with so-called political opponents by abducting them, subjecting them to physical abuse, and holding them in "protective custody" without recourse to the German legal system. In certain regions, the SA and SS even collaborated with German state officials to imprison opponents and undesirables in municipal jails or facilities without any official charges. These "wild" detention camps increased in late February 1933 following the burning of the Reichstag, after which Paul von Hindenburg, the Reich president, issued a decree that suspended civil rights guaranteed by the Weimar Constitution. This development, and the subsequent Enabling Act a few weeks later, giving Hitler and his cabinet sole legislative power, aided the National Socialists in strengthening their grip on the German government. As the National Socialist "revolution" stabilized, many of the smaller temporary camps closed down. Yet some larger camps remained in use and new ones, such as Dachau, opened. As Heinrich Himmler continued to solidify his leadership of the SS, in the summer of 1934, he charged Theodor Eicke, a devout National Socialist and SS member, to oversee the coordination of the concentration camps into a brutal system. By 1937, Eicke had perfected the concentration camp system of terror and ensured its complete control by the SS.[56]

Before the mass roundup of Jews that followed *Kristallnacht*, it is estimated that 5–10 percent of those arrested and interned in concentration camps were Jews. This percentage also included Jewish women, who were placed initially in Moringen concentration camp near Göttingen. No matter what their "crime," Jews were always treated worse than "Aryans" by the police, Gestapo, and SS. Yet, prior to 1935, Jews were generally not incarcerated solely on account of their "race." The SS or Gestapo largely arrested Jews for a variety of other "crimes," such as political opposition or public criticism of National Socialism and, a while later, for returning to Germany after emigrating. Following the promulgation of the Nuremberg Laws in late 1935, Jews were also being arrested for race defilement for engaging in extramarital relations with Aryans. The March 1938 *Anschluss* (annexation of Austria into Germany) further broadened the scope of reasons for the police and Gestapo to harass and arrest enemies of the Reich. Such measures especially affected Austrian Jews. Finally, several months later following *Kristallnacht*, the Gestapo, SS, and police arrested approximately 30,000 Jewish men solely because of their "race." As one historian has concluded, "in the wake of the November Pogrom, the antisemitic motivation for arrest was openly and officially declared."[57]

It was in this climate of increased persecution that Erna wrote in her March 24, 1940, entry, "Jews disappear every day and no one knows what happens to them." She then recalled the tragic plight of her cousins, Herbert and Paul, the sons of her uncle, Daniel. Unfortunately, almost nothing is known about these three individuals beyond what Erna recorded in her diary. Erna revealed that Herbert was placed in a "camp near Leipzig" and Paul, a "decorated World War I veteran," in a "camp near Berlin." It appears that Herbert and Paul were arrested sometime in early 1940 for unspecified reasons.

In addition to the extended family members above, Erna also briefly wrote in her diary about the plight of her cousin, the philologist Dr. Margarete Merzbach, her husband, Dr. Ludwig Merzbach, and their daughter, Uta Merzbach. Dr. Ludwig Merzbach was an auditor in the Berlin economic office of the Reich Association of Jews in Germany (Reichsvereinigung der Juden in Deutschland), an organization forcibly constructed in July 1939 from various remaining Jewish organizations to provide a central means for the SS and Gestapo to communicate with and to control all German Jews. Anyone the Nuremberg Laws defined as Jewish, including Christians of Jewish heritage, was considered a member of the Reichsvereinigung.[58] To ensure the cooperation of the Reichsvereinigung administrators with the German government's forced emigration plans and, after October 1941, with the deportation of German Jews, SS officials had it placed directly under the newly established Reich Main Security Office, or RSHA.[59] Created in September 1939, the RSHA brought together all the security police forces operating in greater Germany and its occupied territories.[60] In June 1943, the RSHA dissolved the Reichsvereinigung and deported its leading members to the Theresienstadt Ghetto. On August 4, 1943, the Merzbach family was transported to Theresienstadt with sixty-seven other Jews.[61] Though the situation in the ghetto was bleak, it was far better than in any of the slave labor camps.[62] In reality, Theresienstadt served only as a temporary dwelling for the Jews deported there, the majority of whom the SS eventually transported farther east to their ultimate deaths.[63] The Merzbach family was particularly fortunate because Ludwig, Margarete, and Uta avoided transport and survived the last months of chaos and rampant disease in Theresienstadt until it was liberated by the Red Army in early

May 1945. By way of Deggendorf, a displaced persons' camp, on May 13, 1946, the Merzbachs departed from Bremen aboard the SS *Marine Perch* bound for New York City.[64] There are no records indicating that the Merzbach family ever reconnected with Erna after the war.

THE ESCALATION OF THE PERSECUTION

OF INTERMARRIED JEWS, 1943–1945

As Erna watched in anguish the persecution and deportation of her German Jewish family members in 1942 and 1943, her own situation grew more precarious as well. As Germany's fortunes waned in the final years of the war, it became clear that the reprieve Hitler had granted to some intermarried Jews was tenuous and temporary. In particular, in the wake of the Wehrmacht's devastating defeat at Stalingrad in February 1943, violent antisemitic propaganda in Germany reached a fever pitch. Joseph Goebbels's propaganda machine launched a vicious campaign in the spring that blamed the escalating war on "World Jewry" bent on destroying "Aryan Humanity."[65] In this time of crisis, the influence of key radicals in Hitler's inner circle, in particular that of Heinrich Himmler of the SS and Martin Bormann of the Party Chancellery, also grew exponentially.[66]

Determined to remove all Jews from Germany, Himmler escalated the persecution of the remaining Jews in Germany, including intermarried Jews. At the end of February 1943, in an operation called the Factory Action (*Fabrikaktion*), the Gestapo arrested and deported to the east most of the approximately 51,000 Jews remaining in Germany. The majority of these Jews were either intermarried or worked as slave laborers in armament factories. The Gestapo rounded up the latter in their places of work and, within days, began to deport them to Auschwitz.[67]

Toward the end of the Factory Action, on March 6, 1943, the Gestapo also arrested Erna in her home. Confronted that spring by intensifying antisemitic rhetoric, she notes that for weeks leading up to the mass arrest of Jews, "I have been living in fear of having my child torn from me as I am deported to one of the infamous camps." After being arrested, Erna spent a terrifying day in the internment camp Grosse Hamburger Strasse in Berlin before being released late that night. Her experience was not unusual—the Gestapo arrested and released most intermarried Jews within days. Historians disagree over the regime's intentions toward intermarried Jews during the Factory Action. In particular, one historian makes a compelling argument that during the Factory Action, the RSHA continued to abide by Hitler's order to exempt intermarried Jews from deportation and arrested them only in order to register them for slave labor assignments.[68]

The Factory Action nonetheless marked an important escalation of the persecution of intermarried Jews. Unable to deport them as a group, the Gestapo began to increasingly target individual intermarried Jews for arrest and deportation on trumped-up criminal charges. An order issued by the Gestapo in Frankfurt an der Oder on the eve of the Factory Action on February 24, 1943, for instance, gave permission to Gestapo agents to counter the "cheeky behavior" of intermarried Jews with arrest and imprisonment in a concentration camp. Agents were encouraged to make "very liberal" use of this policy, as long as they avoided giving the impression that the regime looked to "resolve once and for all the mixed-marriage problem through this action."[69]

Any encounter an intermarried Jew had with a Gestapo agent could mean arrest, imprisonment, and death. When Gestapo agents once again searched the Beckers' home in late March 1943, Erna did not know whether they intended "just" to harass her or to arrest her. Where intermarried Jews lived in the final years of the war could mean the difference between survival and death, as some Gestapo chiefs moved more aggressively against this group of Jews than others. The Gestapo in Frankfurt am Main, for instance, was notorious for its harsh treatment of Jews, including intermarried Jews.[70] Similarly, in Vienna between July 1942 and January 1945, the Gestapo arrested and placed in "protective custody" 139 intermarried Jews on bogus criminal charges.[71] Unlike the majority of Jews, to whom the regime's collective actions, such as decrees and deportation, posed the gravest danger in the final years of the war, the safety and lives of intermarried Jews depended largely on the actions of individuals living with or near them.

THE EMOTIONAL TOLL ON "MIXED"
MARRIAGES IN NAZI GERMANY

First and foremost, intermarried Jews' lives depended on their spouses. A history of the persecution of intermarried Jews is therefore also a history of their intimate partners. Divorce or death of the non-Jewish spouse in a mixed marriage, in particular after the commencement of war, was usually equivalent to a death sentence for the Jewish partner.

Aryan spouses became tainted in the eyes of the regime through their association with their Jewish partners. Even though the Nuremberg Laws only prohibited future marriages between Jewish and non-Jewish Germans, the decree also undermined existing mixed marriages.[72] Erna's jarring opening paragraph of her memoir reflects the accepted sentiment in the Third Reich that although still valid before the law, mixed marriages were nonetheless illicit on account of their fundamental violation of Nazi racial principles: "In March [1938] I am expecting my first child. . . . Both of us will attract much hatred and contempt because I am a Jew and my husband is a race defiler." However, Gustav remained true to his wife and child, even under extreme duress.

In the beginning, Gustav was able to shield his wife from the regime's attacks on Jews that mainly took the form of economic measures against Jewish men. Nevertheless, even then, some intermarried men lost their livelihoods on account of their Jewish wives. For example, a decree dated May 17, 1934, forbade physicians married to non-Aryan spouses from participating in public health insurance.[73] In 1937, the state fired civil servants whose spouses were "not of German or kindred blood."[74]

Many intermarried men who managed to hold on to their jobs nonetheless suffered various forms of discrimination or setbacks in the workplace. In the Protestant Church in Germany, pastors with Jewish wives saw their career prospects vanish.[75] Another example is found as early as 1933, when the inhabitants of Immenhausen in Hesse stopped seeking treatment from their local physicians, the intermarried couple, Drs. Ernst and Lilli Jahn, because Lilli was Jewish. The loss of their medical practice destroyed not just the professional careers of the Jahns but also their private lives.[76]

Unable to legally dissolve all mixed marriages by fiat, the National Socialist government worked to destroy these unions one by one. In 1938, the Nazis passed new legislation to ease the dissolution of mixed marriages. The new marriage law included explicit provisions to dissolve marriages for "racial reasons."[77] The lack of sources makes it difficult to ascertain how many intermarried Germans filed for divorce in Nazi

Germany. Estimates of divorce rates of mixed marriages range from 7 percent to more than 20 percent.[78] After 1941, divorce meant almost certain death for the Jewish partners in mixed marriages. After Ernst Jahn divorced his wife, Lilli, in 1942, she lost her exemption from deportation; Lilli died in Auschwitz sometime in 1944.[79] Though tragic, Lilli Jahn's fate was not the norm—the majority of non-Jewish Germans maintained their loyalty to their Jewish spouses.[80] But the cost of loyalty was high, and Erna's story illuminates how thoroughly the Nazis succeeded in destroying even the lives, marriages, and families of those who might be considered fortunate: the 12,206 intermarried Jews who survived the war and Holocaust in Germany.[81] The relentless persecution and ostracism intermarried couples routinely experienced in Nazi Germany made married life very difficult.

In June 1943, war and persecution forced Erna and Gustav to separate. Erna and her son, Silvan, hastily left Berlin for the remote southern Alpine region of Tyrol and Vorarlberg. They joined millions of evacuees who fled from the escalating Allied bombing war on German cities.[82] As an evacuee, Erna shared an experience common among German women during the Second World War. Her complaints about overcrowding, poor lodging, and frictions between hosts and evacuees echo those of countless women at the time.[83] Unlike most women, though, Erna could not avail herself of the services that the National Socialist People's Welfare Organization and other Nazi party organizations and authorities offered to evacuees.[84] Erna soon realized that although she had escaped the bombing of cities, she had not escaped the worsening persecution of Jews.

Erna and Gustav's marriage started to suffer under the constant strain of separation and worry as local authorities continued to harass and persecute Erna. When the Beckers met in February 1944 in Tannheim, Tyrol, there was little space for intimacy. They were unable to share a room and Gustav fell seriously ill. Soon thereafter, in April 1944, Erna hinted at the toll war and persecution was taking on her marriage and her husband when she wrote: "Gustav has returned to Berlin. He was even more downcast about our wretched situation than I. His pessimism weighed me down, and I can almost cope better on my own." Historians indeed have suggested that in general women coped better than men during the Holocaust.[85]

It commonly was left to women to maintain a semblance of normality for their children amid increasing chaos.[86] Even though her experience was not typical, Erna gives readers an important glimpse of motherhood during the Holocaust. Her insights are valuable because firsthand accounts of mothers and motherhood during the Holocaust are somewhat scarce, in part because women survivors left fewer accounts than men.[87] Moreover, Erna did not mythologize her role as a mother to fit cultural ideals that demanded of mothers unfailing strength, altruism, and self-sacrifice.[88] Rather, against the backdrop of worsening persecution, Erna chronicled episodes of protracted illness, profound exhaustion, and deep despair that barely left her able to care for her son. The theme of threatened or actual separation of mother and child is also prominent throughout the memoir, and Erna lived in anguish that her child might be taken from her by force. At the same time, like many women during the Holocaust, she also had no choice but repeatedly to leave her son with strangers. In 1944, in her darkest hour, Erna convinced herself that Silvan would be better off without his mother altogether, and she attempted suicide. Erna was fortunate, however, to find a number of surrogate mothers for Silvan in southern Germany, who assisted both of them in their most desperate moments.

Although Erna felt safer in rural southern Germany than she had in Berlin, antisemitism was pervasive everywhere. Innsbruck, the Tyrolean capital, was the site of a particularly bloody *Kristallnacht* pogrom, and by 1939, well before Erna settled there, local authorities had driven most local Jews from the area.[89] But soon, the region's Jewish population was on the rise again. Erna was among at least several hundred Jewish refugees who arrived during the war, hoping to hide in the area's remote alpine villages or cross the border into Switzerland. For most, this hope proved elusive. During the war, the Gestapo arrested at least 208 Jewish refugees in Tyrol and Vorarlberg; most perished in Nazi death camps.[90]

However, a number of Jews did survive with the help of the local population. For more than two years, from spring 1943 to the end of the war, the former judge Rudolf Ruhmann and Irene Dann from Berlin and her two daughters hid on numerous Tyrolean farms. Over one hundred locals assisted or knew about these Jewish refugees; no one denounced them to the Gestapo and all four survived the Holocaust.[91]

Although she was not in imminent danger of deportation on account of her privileged status, Nazi authorities often made life unbearable for Erna, and she, too, depended on the aid of locals.

Erna sought refuge and solace in local Catholic communities. Not everyone came to her aid but a considerable number of ordinary Germans, Catholic priests, and nuns did. Often, however, the aid these helpers offered Erna was limited in scope and duration and, time and again, forced her to move on. For this reason, it is not difficult to see why Catholicism and Catholic personages play such a prominent part in Erna's writings, since the aid and protection that rural Catholic communities in southern Germany and Austria offered Erna in the final years of the war, however tenuous and inadequate, were her most important defenses against the Nazi juggernaut. In recounting these many trials of assistance and expulsion in her memoir, Erna may test the patience of some readers. In doing so, however, she illuminates one of the most sinister aspects of Nazi persecution of intermarried Jews. Even though, as pointed out above, Hitler did not permit the deportation and murder of intermarried Jews as a group, his regime intensified their persecution in situ in Germany.

Erna's experiences as a Catholic of Jewish heritage in Hitler's Germany nuances and broadens our understanding of Catholics and the Catholic Church in the Third Reich. The history of the Church has been told primarily from the perspective of the hierarchy, whose silence during the Holocaust was deafening.[92] German bishops even refused to condemn the deportation of Catholics of Jewish heritage.[93] Cardinal Adolf Bertram, the archbishop of Breslau and the head of the Fulda Bishops' Conference, only protested against the regime's plan to dissolve mixed marriages in the summer of 1942 because he viewed it as an infringement of the Church's traditional right to govern marriage.[94]

Catholic priests, nuns, and the laity thus acted on their own initiative and without the hierarchy's support when they aided Jews, including Catholics of Jewish heritage like Erna.[95] Among the many people who assisted Erna, the care and ministry of Father Erwin Röhr, a Dominican, stands out. He first ministered to Erna and her family in Berlin and continued to visit both Silvan and her during their exile in Tyrol. Father Erwin was visiting Erna in June 1944 when, overwhelmed by hopelessness, she attempted suicide.

Suicide rates of German Jews rose dramatically under National Socialism. Like Erna, most Jews who took their own lives did so by consuming poison.[96] There is a debate over the meaning of these deaths suggesting that hopelessness was not necessarily the primary motive in Jewish suicides. As one historian has argued, "Maintaining some sort of dignity was probably a more important motive than pure despair."[97] Nonetheless, it is hard to see Erna's attempted suicide as anything other than an act of despair.[98]

Even in 1944 and 1945, as Allied forces closed in on Germany, the regime did not abandon the Final Solution. On the contrary, it intensified the persecution of mixed marriages when it increased the pressure on intermarried Aryan men to divorce their Jewish spouses. The Nazis considered Aryan men married to Jewish women as *wehrunwürdig*, meaning they were unworthy of serving in the German armed forces.[99] In October 1943, Hitler decreed the conscription of these men into work battalions of the Organization Todt (OT), a civil engineering organization founded by Fritz Todt, a longtime member of the National Socialist Party.[100] In March 1944, there was a second attempt to draft "defense unworthy" men into the OT.[101] It is unclear how many men were affected by these first two actions, but it appears that many were able to evade the order with the help of their employers who routinely and vehemently fought the loss of qualified personnel.[102]

By October 1944, amid the regime's frenzied, final attempt to mobilize the entire German population for the war effort, the RSHA refused to consider any further exemptions. That fall, RSHA officials ordered the transfer of all able-bodied "Jewish persons of mixed blood of the first degree" and Aryan men married to Jewish women from their place of employment to labor camps in the OT.[103] Following the failed attempt on Hitler's life in July 1944, the RSHA was able to expand its powers even further.[104] In these final months of the Second World War, the RSHA targeted all Aryan men married to Jewish women for forced labor in a brutal last-ditch effort to compel them to divorce their wives.[105]

In October 1944, Erna received the devastating news of her husband's imminent internment in a labor camp. Racked by guilt that Gustav had to endure imprisonment on her account, she risked the perilous journey through war-torn Germany to see her husband off as he entered a camp near Berlin. Degraded to a forced worker, Gustav had to perform hard physical labor in the chemical plant, Leunawerke, near Halle, Germany. Erna had no choice but to return to Tyrol, where local authorities mercilessly chased her and her son from place to place. Her situation became truly dire when, on February 14, 1945, the RSHA ordered intermarried Jews throughout Germany to report for labor deployment at a designated place and date.[106]

The order for labor deployment was a ruse. Even as Germany faced certain and imminent defeat, in the spring of 1945, the RSHA made one final attempt to deport all Jews, including those in mixed marriages. In the months between February and April 1945, the RSHA oversaw nineteen separate deportations from Germany to Theresienstadt.[107] Fortunately, in the chaos of the final months of the war, many intermarried Jews managed to evade the order for their deportation. It appears that Erna did not even receive the order, which is not surprising since she was constantly on the move. Nonetheless, she was well aware of the continued and even heightened danger to her life in these final months and weeks of the war. As late as April 1945, Erna surmised that she was "in a race with freedom," and she wondered whether the Americans would reach her in time. Once again, in this last phase of the war, intermarried Jews' lives depended on the actions of local officials. Fortunately, the police and local officials Erna encountered were mostly content with chasing her and her son out of town. In the face of certain defeat, even some Gestapo agents became less zealous in pursuit of their duty. In Munich in the spring of 1945, for example, the local Gestapo exempted most intermarried Jews from deportation, even though they had no authority to do so.[108]

As late as April 1945, a local farmer denounced Erna as a Jew to Josef Oettl, the local party leader of Pettnau. Despite receiving this information, Oettl refused to act on it because Erna "surely had not harmed anyone." In other places, local officials took a much tougher stance, and authorities deported at least one intermarried Jewish woman from nearby Oberstdorf, near Sonthofen.[109] In a small town near Regensburg, an SS officer shot an intermarried Jewish man in the final days of the war in what was presumably an act of revenge.[110] American troops did not arrive in Pettnau until the first week of May. Only then did Erna know

with certainty that she and Silvan had survived the war and Nazi persecution. The German government officially surrendered to the Allied
forces a few days later on May 7, 1945.

Erna was free, but she could not rejoice. Only in the chaos of the immediate postwar period, as she learned of the death of most of her large
Jewish family, did she begin to comprehend the scale of her loss and
despair. For eight months after liberation, Erna also had no news of Gustav. By October 1945, she had little hope that he was still alive. Without
family, Erna and Silvan became part of the roughly 3 million wartime
evacuees who did not return to their prewar homes after the war ended.[111]
After Gustav's return in January 1946, the Beckers joined the ranks of
those for whom, as one scholar wrote, displacement became "a more
lasting condition and coming home was a disappointment, or worse."[112]
During his time of imprisonment, Gustav contracted a debilitating and
life-threatening case of skeletal tuberculosis. He succumbed to his illness in March 1952.

Erna was far from a "fortunate" survivor, and her memoir illuminates
the price the Nazis demanded for her life. Hitler was willing to make
certain concessions to intermarried Jews to address the more immediate
concerns of appeasing the churches and parts of the German public.[113]
These concessions, however, did not mean that the Nazis had lost sight
of their goal of killing all Jews, but meant that in the case of intermarried
Jews they were willing to accept certain delays. In the meantime, and
with the help of ordinary Germans, the regime decentralized the persecution of intermarried Jews and their spouses, hoping that the latter
would divorce their partners. Most, like Gustav, refused. His love for
Erna served as a rampart and defense against her deportation to and
eventual death at Auschwitz. In the end, it was Gustav, not Erna, who
was pulled into the maelstrom of a murderous regime that was already
in its final death throes. The Nazis thus exacted full payment for Erna's
survival: her home, her marriage, and her faithful husband's life.

NOTES

1. Erna's father, Heinrich Kohen, was born on December 23, 1868, in the French–
German border town of Schlettstadt in the Alsace region. The French town of
Sélestat became Schlettstadt when it was annexed to Germany following the

Franco-Prussian War of 1870–1871. It returned to France following the First World War (1914–1918). Erna's mother, Isabella David, was born on May 26, 1871, in Kobern an der Mosel near Koblenz, Germany. She died on April 11, 1943.

2. Erna Becker-Kohen, "Nachwort," in *Wer die Wege kennt* (Freiburg im Breisgau: Karl Schillinger, 1980), 157–159.

3. This figure corresponds to the first census data available in 1939. On this point, see Beate Meyer, *"Jüdische Mischlinge": Rassenpolitik und Verfolgunserfahrung 1933–1945* (Munich: Dölling & Galitz, 1999), 25. On mixed marriages in Nazi Germany, see also Ursula Büttner, *Die Not der Juden teilen: Christlich-jüdische Familien im Dritten Reich: Beispiel und Zeugnis des Schriftstellers Robert Brendel* (Hamburg: Hans Christians, 1988); Nathan Stoltzfus, *Resistance of the Heart: Intermarriage and the Rosenstrasse Protest in Nazi Germany* (New Brunswick, NJ: Rutgers University Press, 2001); and Evan Burr Bukey, *Jews and Intermarriage in Nazi Austria* (Cambridge: Cambridge University Press, 2011). For works on "persons of mixed blood," see Meyer, *"Jüdische Mischlinge"*; Jeremy Noakes, "The Development of Nazi Policy towards the German-Jewish 'Mischlinge' 1933–1945," *Leo Baeck Institute Year Book* 34 (1989): 291–354; and James F. Trent, *In the Shadow of the Holocaust: Nazi Persecution of Jewish-Christian Germans* (Lawrence: University Press of Kansas, 2003).

4. Führererlass vom 28. Dezember, in *Dokumente über die Verfolgung der jüdischen Bürger in Baden-Württemberg durch das nationalsozialistische Regime 1933–1943*, part 2, ed. Paul Sauer (Stuttgart: Kohlhammer, 1966), 83–84. On this point, see also Wolf Gruner, *Widerstand in der Rosenstrasse: Die Fabrikaktion und die Verfolgung der "Mischehen" 1943* (Frankfurt am Main: Fischer, 2005), 83–84; and Maximilian Strnad, "The Fortune of Survival: Intermarried German Jews in the Dying Breath of the 'Thousand-Year Reich,'" *Dapien: Studies on the Holocaust* 29 (2015): 173–196.

5. Meyer, *"Jüdische Mischlinge,"* 30.

6. Büttner, *Die Not der Juden teilen*, 8.

7. Erna Becker-Kohen, "Das Tagebuch von Frau Erna Becker-Kohen, 1937–1963" (New York: Center for Jewish History, Leo Baeck Institute, 1976).

8. Steven Kagle, *American Diary Literature 1620–1799* (Boston: Twayne, 1979), 15.

9. Lawrence Langer, *Holocaust Testimonies: The Ruins of Memory* (New Haven, CT: Yale University Press, 1991), 41.

10. Ibid. As Annette Wieviorka has also noted, historians are often suspect of testimonies composed years after the event because "particularly when they are produced as part of a larger cultural movement, [they] express the discourse or discourses valued by society at the moment the witnesses tell their stories as much as they render the individual experience." Annette Wieviorka, *The Era of the Witness* (Ithaca, NY: Cornell University Press, 2006), xii. Na'am Shik, too, was suspicious of the effect time had on survivor accounts when she wrote, "Women's and men's testimonies and writings from the immediate postwar period constitute a historical source of great importance. In them the horrors, the difficulties, and the various abuses appear in a far more blatant and less 'literary' manner than in later writings.

Their descriptions are laconic, emotionally 'flat,' lacking what could be called 'philosophical' musings." Na'ama Shik, "Infinite Loneliness: Some Aspects of the Lives of Jewish Women in the Auschwitz Camps according to Testimonies and Autobiographies Written between 1945 and 1948," in *Lessons and Legacies*, vol. 8, *From Generation to Generation*, ed. Doris Bergen (Evanston, IL: Northwestern University Press, 2008), 127.

11. Walter Dirks, "Vorwort," in Becker-Kohen, *Wer die Wege kennt*, 14–15.

12. Ibid.

13. *Badische Zeitung*, November 18, 1958.

14. For example, see Marion A. Kaplan, *Between Dignity and Despair: Jewish Life in Nazi Germany* (New York: Oxford University Press, 1998); Gruner, *Widerstand in der Rosenstrasse*; Jana Leichsenring, *Die katholische Kirche und "ihre" Juden: Das "Hilfswerk beim Bischöflichen Ordinariat Berlin," 1938–1945* (Berlin: Metropol, 2007); Nicholas Stargardt, *The German War: A Nation under Arms, 1939–1945* (New York: Basic Books, 2015); and Frederick S. Roden, *Recovering Jewishness: Modern Identities Reclaimed* (Santa Barbara, CA: Praeger, 2016).

15. Avishai Margalit, *The Ethics of Memory* (Cambridge, MA: Harvard University Press, 2002), 150. For a discussion of the Holocaust survivor as a "moral witness," see Siegrun Bubser Wildner, "Hybrid Testimony and Moral Indictment: A Survivor's Poetic Response to the Mauthausen Nazi Concentration Camp Experience," *Holocaust and Genocide Studies* 29 (2015): 460–477.

16. Becker-Kohen, "Nachwort," 158.

17 Ibid.

18. Adolf Hitler, *Mein Kampf*, trans. Ralph Mannheim (Boston: Houghton Mifflin, 1999), 284–329.

19. Section 3.2 of the law declared, "Section 1 does not apply to civil servants in office from August 1, 1914, who fought at the Front for the German Reich or its Allies in the World War, or whose fathers or sons fell in the World War. Other exceptions may be permitted by the Reich Minister of the Interior in coordination with the Minister concerned or with the highest authorities with respect to civil servants working abroad." See Law for the Restoration of the Professional Civil Service, April 7, 1933, in *Documents on the Holocaust: Selected Sources on the Destruction of the Jews of Germany and Austria, Poland, and the Soviet Union*, 8th ed., ed. Yitzhak Arad, Israel Gutman, and Abraham Margaliot, trans. Lea Ben Dor (Lincoln: University of Nebraska Press and Yad Vashem, 1999), 39–41, here 40.

20. The "Aryan Paragraph" can actually be found in the First Ordinance on the Implementation of the Law for the Restoration of the Professional Civil Service,of April 11, 1933, in Arad, Gutman, and Margaliot, *Documents on the Holocaust*, 41–42.

21. Büttner, *Die Note der Juden teilen*, 13; Meyer, "Jüdische Mischlinge," 30.

22. For a text of the Nuremberg laws of September 15, 1935, and the subsequent first regulation to it of November 14, 1935, see Arad, Gutman, and Margaliot, *Documents on the Holocaust*, 77–80.

23. For example, see Robert Gellately, *The Gestapo and German Society: Enforcing Racial Policy 1933–1945* (Oxford: Clarendon, 1992); and Michael Wildt, *Hitlers Volksgemesinchaft and the Dynamics of Racial Exclusion: Violence against Jews in Provincial Germany, 1919–1939*, trans. Bernard Heise (New York: Berghahn Books in association with Yad Vashem, 2012).

24. On October 24, 1941, the regime published a decree that made any public display of sympathy for Jews illegal. Anyone who violated the decree risked three months' imprisonment in a concentration camp. Stargardt, *The German War*, 242.

25. Kaplan, *Between Dignity and Despair*, 20.

26. For an overview of the events leading up to and during *Kristallnacht*, including an examination of the role ordinary non-Jewish Germans played in it, see Alan Steinweis, *Kristallnacht 1938* (Cambridge, MA: Harvard University Press, 2009).

27. On this point, see Peter Longerich, *Holocaust: The Nazi Persecution and Murder of the Jews* (New York: Oxford University Press, 2010), 134.

28. Hitler, *Mein Kampf*, 286.

29. Gruner, *Widerstand in der Rosenstrasse*, 91–94.

30. Protocol of the Wannsee Conference, January 20, 1942, in Arad, Gutman, and Margaliot, *Documents on the Holocaust*, 249–261.

31. Gruner, *Widerstand in der Rosenstrasse*, 91.

32. According to the census of May 17, 1939, there existed a total of 4,586 mixed marriages between non-Jewish German men and Jewish German women "not of the Jewish faith," the majority of whom were presumably Christian. In addition, there were 3,551 mixed marriages between non-Jewish German women and Jewish men "not of the Jewish faith." See Noakes, "The Development of Nazi Policy," 297.

33. On the Catholic Church and intermarried Jews, see Jana Leichsenring, "Katholiken in der Rosenstrasse. Das 'Hilfswerk beim Bischöflichen Ordinariat Berlin' und die 'Mischehen,'" *Zeitschrift für Geschichtswissenschaften* 52 (2004): 37–49. On the regime's apparent unwillingness to alienate Aryan relatives of intermarried Jews, see Meyer, *"Jüdische Mischlinge,"* 27.

34. Gruner, *Widerstand in der Rosenstrasse*, 91–94; Leichsenring, "Katholiken in der Rosenstrasse."

35. Konrad Kwiet, "Without Neighbors: Daily Living in *Judenhäuser*," in *Jewish Life in Nazi Germany: Dilemmas and Responses*, ed. Francis R. Nicosia and David Scrase (New York: Berghahn Books, 2010), 117–148, here 126–127.

36. On the rise of emigration after November 1938, see Herbert A. Strauss, "Jewish Emigration from Germany: Nazi Policies and Jewish Responses. Part I," in *The Nazi Holocaust: Historical Articles on the Destruction of European Jews*, part 8, *Bystanders to the Holocaust*, vol. 1, ed. Michael R. Marrus (Westport, CT: Meckler, 1989), 161–206.

37. Debórah Dwork and Robert Jan van Pelt, *Flight from the Reich: Refugee Jews, 1933–1946* (New York: Norton, 2009), 97–103.

38. Martin Dean, *Robbing the Jews: The Confiscation of Jewish Property in the Holocaust, 1933–1945* (New York: Cambridge University Press in association with

the United States Holocaust Memorial Museum, 2008), 77–78; and Kaplan, *Between Dignity and Despair*, 129–132.

39. Herbert A. Strauss, "Jewish Emigration from Germany: Nazi Policies and Jewish Responses. Part II," in *The Nazi Holocaust: Historical Articles on the Destruction of European Jews*, part 8, *Bystanders to the Holocaust*, vol. 3, ed. Michael R. Marrus (Westport, CT: Meckler, 1989), 1415–1481, here 1447–1451.

40. On the history of Chile and Jewish immigration during the Holocaust, see Eva Goldschmidt Wyman, *Escaping Hitler: A Jewish Haven in Chile* (Tuscaloosa: University of Alabama Press, 2013), esp. 74–85 and 101–107.

41. United States Holocaust Memorial Museum (hereafter USHMM), "German Jewish Refugees, 1933–1939," *Holocaust Encyclopedia*, http://www.ushmm.org/wlc /en/article.php?ModuleId=10005468.

42. Jeremy Noakes and Geoffrey Pridham, *Nazism 1919–1945: A Documentary Reader*, vol. 3, *Foreign Policy, War and Racial Extermination*, rev. ed. (Exeter: University of Exeter Press, 2006), 520–521.

43. Yehuda Bauer, *American Jewry and the Holocaust: The American Jewish Joint Distribution Committee, 1939–1945* (Detroit: Wayne State University Press in association with the Institute for Contemporary Jewry, Hebrew University, Jerusalem, 1981), 66.

44. On the impact of the war on emigration, see Michael Schäbitz, "The Flight and Expulsion of German Jews," in *Jews in Nazi Berlin: From Kristallnacht to Liberation*, ed. Beate Meyer, Hermann Simon, and Chana Schütz, trans. Caroline Gay and Miranda Robbins (Chicago: University of Chicago Press, 2009), 36–62, esp. 53–59.

45. Marcel Bervoets-Tragholz, *La liste de Saint-Cyprien: L'odyssée de plusieurs milliers de Juifs expulsés le 10 mai 1940 par les autorités belges vers les camps d'internement du Sud de la France, antichambre des camps d'extermination* (Brussels: Alice Éditions, 2006), 375.

46. Ibid., 124–125; and Anne Grynberg, *Les camps de la honte: Les internés juifs des camps français 1939–1944* (Paris: Éditions la Découverte, 1991), 81.

47. Bervoets-Tragholz, *La liste de Saint-Cyprien*, 375.

48. Max Kohen was assigned to block 1, barrack 25. See ibid., 220.

49. For a vivid description of life in the camp, see Otto Schrag and Peter Schrag, *When Europe Was a Prison Camp: Father and Son Memories 1940–1941* (Bloomington: Indiana University Press, 2015).

50. On Saint-Cyprien and the other French camps, see Denis Peschanski, *La france des camps: L'internement, 1938–1946* (Paris: Gallimard, 2002), esp. 98–147.

51. Max Kohen, Gurs registration card, USHMM, RG-43.035M, Reel 51, Selected records from the Departmental Archives of the Pyrenees-Atlantiques, 1912–1953 (500W, Camp de Gurs). Kohen was assigned to subcamp C, building 1H.

52. Ibid. A handwritten note on Max Kohen's Gurs registration card records the transfer camp and date.

53. On the turnover and the role of Drancy transit camp, see Grynberg, *Les camps de la honte*, 310–318, esp. 316.

54. Deportation List of the 25th Transport from Drancy to Auschwitz, 1.1.9.1/11180932/ITS Digital Archive, USHMM; and the Transport list of those deported from Drancy to Auschwitz on August 28, 1942, 1.1.9.9/11188410/ITS Digital Archive, USHMM. See also Serge Klarsfeld, *Memorial to the Jews Deported from France 1942–1944: A Documentation of the Deportation of the Victims of the Final Solution in France* (New York: Beate Klarsfeld Foundation, 1983), 218–222.

55. For a brief but insightful discussion of the distinction between the two, see Nikolaus Wachsmann, *KL: A History of the Nazi Concentration Camps* (New York: Farrar, Straus and Giroux, 2015), 322–325.

56. For a succinct overview of the evolution of the camps, see Nikolaus Wachsmann, "The Dynamics of Destruction: The Development of the Concentration Camps, 1933–1945," in *Concentration Camps in Nazi Germany: The New Histories*, ed. Jane Caplan and Nikolaus Wachsmann (New York: Routledge, 2010), 17–43. On Dachau, see Christopher Dillon, *Dachau and the SS: A Schooling in Violence* (New York: Oxford University Press, 2015), esp. 175–178.

57. Kim Wünschmann, *Before Auschwitz: Jewish Prisoners in the Prewar Concentration Camps* (Cambridge, MA: Harvard University Press, 2015), 51, 69, 105–113, 199.

58. On the history of the Reichsvereinigung, see Beate Meyer, *A Fatal Balancing Act: The Dilemma of the Reich Association of Jews in Germany, 1939–1945*, trans. William Templer (New York: Berghahn Books, 2011), esp. 23–30. On Dr. Ludwig Merzbach, see 182–183, 190–191, 226, 239.

59. On the deportation of German Jews, see Alfred Gottwaldt and Diana Schulle, *Die "Judendeportationen" aus dem Deutschen Reich 1941–1945* (Wiesbaden: Marix, 2005); and Birthe Kundrus and Beate Meyer, eds., *Die Deportation der Juden aus Deutschland: Pläne, Praxis, Reaktionen 1938–1945. Beitrage zur Geschichte des Nationalsozialismus*, vol. 20, 2nd ed. (Göttingen: Wallstein, 2005).

60. On the establishment of the RSHA, see Michael Wildt, *An Uncompromising Generation: The Nazi Leadership of the Reich Security Main Office*, trans. Tom Lampert (Madison: University of Wisconsin Press, 2009), esp. 125–164.

61. Gestapo Transport list transcribed on April 4, 1944: 95th *Alterstransport* deported on August 4, 1943, 1.2.1.1./11194093/ITS Digital Archive, USHMM. Ludwig, Margarete, and Uta Merzbach are listed as numbers 62, 63, and 64, respectively.

62. On the conditions in Theresienstadt, see Philipp Manes, *As If It Were Life: A WWII Diary from the Theresienstadt Ghetto*, ed. Ben Barkow and Klaus Leist, trans. Janet Foster, Ben Barkow, and Klaus Leist (New York: Palgrave Macmillan, 2009); and Norbert Troller, *Theresienstadt: Hitler's Gift to the Jews*, trans. Susan E. Cernyak-Spatz (Chapel Hill: University of North Carolina Press, 1991). On Theresienstadt in general, see Livia Rothkirchen, *The Jews of Bohemia and Moravia* (Lincoln: University of Nebraska Press and Yad Vashem, 2005), esp. 233–283.

63. There were sixty-three transports "totaling more than 87,000 people from Terezín. Aside from Riga, deportees were sent to ghettos including Białystock, Łódź, Minsk, Piaski Luterskie, and Warsaw and to concentration camps and extermination centers at Auschwitz II–Birkenau, Lublin-Majdanek, and Treblinka. Approximately 3,800 of them survived the war." Voktĕch Blodig and Joseph Robert White, "Terezín," in *The United States Holocaust Memorial Museum Encyclopedia of Camps and Ghettos, 1933–1945*, vol. 2, *Ghettos in German-Occupied Eastern Europe*, part A, ed. Martin Dean (Bloomington: Indiana University Press in association with the United States Holocaust Memorial Museum, 2012), 180–184, here 181.

64. Second List of 331 persons who desire to go abroad from Terezin-Theresienstadt, 1.1.42.1/4956071/ITS Digital Archive, USHMM. Compiled on July 16, 1945, Ludwig, Margarete, and Uta Merzbach are listed as numbers 86, 87, and 88, respectively. List of the inhabitants at Deggendorf Displaced Persons camp, issued on January 1, 1946, 3.1.1.2/81974894/ITS Digital Archive, USHMM. List of the inhabitants at Deggendorf Displaced Persons camp, Passenger Manifest of the SS *Marine Perch*, May 13, 1946, 3.1.3.2/81649764/ITS Digital Archive, USHMM. The SS *Marine Perch* left Bremen for New York City on May 13, 1946.

65. Stargardt, *The German War*, 364.

66. Ibid., 334–335.

67. According to Wolf Gruner, in 1943, 20,406 of the 51,327 Jews remaining in Germany were forced laborers. Gruner, *Widerstand in der Rosenstrasse*, 46, 71–75.

68. Wolf Gruner cites instructions issued by the RSHA on February 20, 1943, which outline new guidelines for the "evacuation" of Jews to the east. The guidelines explicitly exempt Jews living in a "German-Jewish mixed marriage." See Gruner, *Widerstand in der Rosenstrasse*, 50–52. Lending further credence to this argument is the denial of a request made in January 1943 by the NSDAP (Nazi Party) district leader (*Kreisleiter*) of Rostock, Otto Dettmann, to deport the remaining twenty Jews in his district, all of whom were intermarried. Strnad, "The Fortune of Survival," 176. By contrast, Nathan Stoltzfus disagrees, arguing that the regime only released Jewish husbands of non-Jewish wives after the latter protested outside of the Rosenstrasse transit camp in the spring of 1943. Stoltzfus, *Resistance of the Heart*.

69. Gruner, *Widerstand in der Rosenstrasse*, 53.

70. In Frankfurt am Main, the local gauleiter, Jakob Sprenger, demanded that officials move aggressively against remaining Jews and denounce them to the Gestapo for "the most minor transgressions." In one such case, the Gestapo arrested a Jewish woman because she wrote in pencil on her identification card. See Gruner, *Widerstand in der Rosenstrasse*, 173.

71. Burkey, *Jews and Intermarriage in Nazi Austria*, 152.

72. The preamble to the Law for the Protection of German Blood and Honor (September 15, 1935) reads as follows: "Moved by the understanding that purity of German blood is the essential condition for the continued existence of the German people, and inspired by the inflexible determination to ensure the existence of the German nation for all time, the Reichstag has unanimously adopted the following

law," which forbade marriages between Jews and non-Jews. See Nuremberg Law for the Protection of German Blood and German Honor, September 15, 1935, in Arad, Gutman, and Margaliot, *Documents on the Holocaust*, 78–79.

73. According to the May 17, 1934, decree concerning admittance of doctors to Germany's health insurance system, it was "sufficient if one parent or one grandparent is non-Aryan." Verordnung über die Zulassung von Ärzten zur Tätigkeit bei den Krankenkassen vom 17. Mai 1934, *Reichsgesetzblatt* (RGBl), 1934, Part I, 399–410, here 401.See also Michael Burleigh and Wolfgang Wippermann, *The Racial State: Germany 1933–1945*, 16th ed. (Cambridge: Cambridge University Press, 2009), 80.

74. Deutsches Beamtengesetz vom 26. Januar 1937, RGBl, 1937, Part I, 41–70, here 50.

75. In September 1933, the journalist and writer Jochen Klepper recorded in his diary that his friend Kurt Meschke could not remain in his post as student pastor in Danzig on account of his Jewish wife and was searching for a new position in a small Pomeranian parish. See Jochen Klepper, *Unter den Schatten deiner Flügel: Aus den Tagebüchern der Jahre 1932 bis 1942* (Stuttgart: Deutsche Verlags-Anstalt, 1971), 88.

76. Thomas Kühne, *Belonging and Genocide: Hitler's Community, 1918–1945* (New Haven, CT: Yale University Press, 2010), 39.

77. See section 37 of the July 6, 1938, decree for the standardization of the rights of marriage and divorce in the provinces of Austria and in the rest of the territory of the Reich, RGBl, 1938, Part I, 807. See also Meyer, *"Jüdische Mischlinge,"* 69.

78. Ursula Büttner cites the example of Baden-Württemberg during the Nazi era where 97 (7.2 percent) out of 1,355 intermarried couples divorced. Büttner, *Die Not der Juden teilen*, 298. In the absence of concrete sources, Evan Burr Burkey concluded that 7 percent, or 394, Viennese intermarried couples may have divorced between 1938 and 1945. See Burkey, *Jews and Intermarriage in Nazi Austria*, 95. Beate Meyer based her analysis on 130 available divorce proceedings of intermarried couples in Hamburg between 1938 and 1945. Even though divorce statistics for 1933 to 1938 are not available, Meyer estimates that the divorce rate of mixed marriages exceeded 20 percent. Meyer, *"Jüdische Mischlinge,"* 73.

79. Kühne, *Belonging and Genocide*, 40.

80. Statistics on Jews who survived the Holocaust in Germany reveal the importance of intermarriage in survival. According to Maximillian Strnad, in 1945 "12,206 of the 14,288 Jews still living in Germany proper (*Altreich*) were intermarried." See Strnad, "The Fortune of Survival," 174.

81. Ibid. The number does not include their partners.

82. As of January 11, 1945, there were approximately 8.9 million German evacuees. The vast majority, 6.2 million, had fled the bombing war. Most were women and children. In the case of Munich, only 10 percent of the city's 200,000 evacuees were men. See Nicole Kramer, *Volksgenossinnen an der Heimatfront: Mobilisierung, Verhalten, Erinnerung* (Göttingen: Vandenhoeck & Ruprecht, 2011), 278, 283.

83. Ibid., 285–293.

84. Ibid., 279–293.

85. Esther Hertzog, "Introduction: Studying the Holocaust as a Feminist," in *Life, Death and Sacrifice: Women and Family in the Holocaust*, ed. Esther Hertzog (Jerusalem: Gefen Publishing House, 2008), 2.

86. On this point, see Kaplan, *Between Dignity and Despair*, 50–73.

87. Dalia Ofer, "Motherhood under Siege," in Hertzog, *Life, Death and Sacrifice*, 42.

88. Ibid., 43.

89. The Jewish population of Tyrol and Vorarlberg was small, consisting of approximately 660 Jews. By September 1939, at least 440 Jews had left the area. But Thomas Albrich believes that the actual number of Jews who fled Tyrol and Vorarlberg was actually higher. See Thomas Albrich, " 'Die Juden hinaus' aus Tirol und Vorarlberg: Entrechtung und Vertreibung 1938–1940," in *Tirol und Vorarlberg in der NS-Zeit*, ed. Rolf Steininger and Sabine Pitscheider (Innsbruck: Studien, 2002), 299, 301, 311.

90. Thomas Albrich, "Die 'Endlösung der Judenfrage' im Gau Tirol-Vorarlberg und Vernichtung 1941 bis 1945," in Steininger and Pitscheider, *Tirol und Vorarlberg*, 353.

91. Ibid., 352.

92. On this point, for example, see Olaf Blaschke, *Die Kirchen und der Nationalsozialismus* (Ditzingen: Reclam, 2014); Michael Phayer, *The Catholic Church and the Holocaust, 1930–1965* (Bloomington: Indiana University Press, 2000); and Robert A. Ventresca, *Soldier of Christ: The Life of Pope Pius XII* (Cambridge, MA: Belknap Press of Harvard University Press, 2014).

93. The Catholic Church did attempt to assist Catholics of Jewish heritage with emigration and matters through an organization called the Relief Agency of the Berlin Chancery (Hilfswerk beim Bischöflichen Ordinariat Berlin), which was established in 1938 by Konrad Graf von Preysing, bishop of Berlin. Starting in the summer of 1941, the Relief Agency's director, Margarete Sommer, sent the first of several urgent reports to Cardinal Adolf Bertram, chairman of the Fulda Conference of Catholic Bishops, which detailed the Nazis' deportation and murder of Jews, including Catholics of Jewish heritage. See Leichsenring, "Katholiken in der Rosenstrasse," 38–49. For a history of the Relief Agency, see Leichsenring, *Die katholische Kirche und "ihre" Juden*. On Sommer, see Michael Phayer, *Protestant and Catholic Women in Nazi Germany* (Detroit: Wayne State University Press, 1990), esp. 204–224.

94. Leichsenring, "Katholiken in der Rosenstrasse," 42.

95. On this point, see Kevin P. Spicer, *Resisting the Third Reich: The Catholic Clergy in Hitler's Berlin* (DeKalb: Northern Illinois University Press, 2004), 120–138.

96. Christian Goeschel writes, "In 1937, the Berlin Jewish community was so worried about the growing number of suicides that it commissioned a study for it. . . . Whereas in 1924–1926, there had been around 50.4 suicides per 100,000 Jews living in Berlin, these levels had increased in 1932–1934 when there were 70.2 suicides per 100,000." Once the Nazis began deporting Jews to the East in the fall of 1941, suicide rates of Jews increased even further. Between late 1940 to late 1941, Jewish suicides rose by 516 percent. In the fall of 1942 in Berlin, when Jews comprised

a tiny fraction of the city's population, 481 out of 669 suicides were Jewish. See Christian Goeschel, *Suicide in Nazi Germany* (Oxford: Oxford University Press, 2009), 100, 107–109.

97. Ibid., 117.

98. Although the regime tried to stop Jews scheduled for deportation from committing suicide, prior to the start of deportations the Nazis welcomed Jewish suicides as a means to rid the country of Jews. Christian Goeschel cites numerous examples of the Nazi regime's brutal treatment of Jewish suicides. For example, in 1938 in Vienna, "After a Jewish shopkeeper had committed suicide together with his family, storm troopers plastered his shop window with placards saying 'Please imitate.'" Ibid., 101.

99. On April 8, 1940, Wilhelm Keitel, chief of the supreme command of the German armed forces, issued a secret decree concerning the treatment of Jewish persons of mixed blood in the armed forces that ordered the dismissal from the armed forces of Jewish persons of mixed blood of the first degree and men married to Jews or to Jewish persons of mixed blood. See H. G. Adler, *Der Verwaltete Mensch: Studien zur Deportation der Juden aus Deutschland* (Tübingen: Mohr Siebeck, 1974), 295.

100. Dieter Maier, *Arbeitseinsatz und Deportation: Die Mitwirkung der Arbeitsverwaltung bei der nationalsozialistischen Judenverfolgung in den Jahren 1938–1945* (Berlin: Hentrich, 1994), 217.

101. Ibid., 219.

102. Ibid., 221.

103. Ibid., 225.

104. Stargardt, *The German War*, 455.

105. Strnad, "The Fortune of Survival," 194.

106. Büttner, *Die Not der Juden teilen*, 69.

107. This number corresponds to 13.3 percent of Jews registered in Germany. Strnad, "The Fortune of Survival," 188.

108. Ibid., 186.

109. The woman's name was Eva Noak-Mosse. On February 20, 1945, she was deported to Theresienstadt concentration camp. Ibid., 187.

110. Ibid., 189.

111. Stargardt, *The German War*, 549.

112. Ian Buruma, *Year Zero: A History of 1945* (New York: Penguin, 2013), 133.

113. On this point, see Nathan Stoltzfus, *Hitler's Compromises: Coercion and Consensus in Nazi Germany* (New Haven, CT: Yale University Press, 2016).

≈

THE MEMOIR OF

Erna Becker-Kohen

CHRISTMAS 1937

In March I am expecting my first child. I will embrace it as a gift from God. But how will its life unfold? Both of us will attract much hatred and contempt because I am a Jew and my husband is a race defiler. Although he remains true to me because he loves me so very much, even he will not be able to change the fact that people will reject not just me but his child as well. May God give this child a big, loving heart because only then will it be able to bear the hostile world.

Yet, how different the world appears to me now. I was in such despair, so full of fear until I recognized that a great task was awaiting me, and I want to fulfill it.

MARCH 23, 1938

Our little Silvan was baptized today in our small parish church.[1] A Jesuit priest performed the sacred rites. Little Silvan, from the moment I first felt you stir under my heart you have been my light and guide. The weeks of awaiting the hour of your birth so full of anticipation were the most blessed and beautiful of my life. How I recognized the wise hand of a merciful God when I felt your little beating heart. Now you are here! May God use me as His tool to do what is good and noble.

33

CHRISTMAS 1938

I have never experienced the magic of Christmas as I did today, next to our boy, whose eyes almost outshined the candles on the Christmas tree. Each light is a miracle, the Christ child in the crib a dear brother. O sweet peace, remain!

APRIL 1939

At the parental home in Frankfurt. We risked the long journey by car with our small boy. Happy days for Gustav and his mother.[2] For Silvan, too, there are many new things to see.

For me it was a sad homecoming. My mother,[3] driven from her home, was given a shabby room for just a few days.[4] Fear radiates from her sad, kind eyes. How that upsets me. Where can she go? Is there not one single good soul left in this vast city? Who will take pity on the Jew, this person of a different race? With great bitterness she tells me once again that her great-grandfather was a vintner in the Moselle region, respected and revered by everyone. My father, who passed away long ago, was also a Jew from an Alsatian family of scholars. But now we are to be "aliens." We have become homeless. My sister is packing her last belongings. She and her husband plan on emigrating to Chile next month where they want to build a new life together. Ruth will persevere. She is a dentist, intelligent and resolute. But I do worry about my brother. For two years now he has been living in Brussels. Will he be able to create a new home for himself there? The historian, the quiet academic will have a difficult time. He wants to take in mother.

After much searching I found a place for mother. With much love, the sisters of St. Vincent de Paul took in this woman of a faith different from their own, and they care for her despite the great danger it exposes them to.[5] May God in Heaven reward them for it. Poor mother! She is so full of fear and completely intimidated.

For days on end I wander aimlessly through the city in a vain search for peace among its old lanes and alleyways. There is little empathy for my plight in my mother-in-law's home. One would expect nothing less from good Germans. My Jewish classmates and teachers have emigrated or disappeared, and I can't burden my husband Gustav with my family's problems. I am safe after all on account of his Aryan ancestry.

I can no longer bear the misery here. Every day we hear of new attacks on Jews. Does anyone even ask questions? Everything the Führer orders must be right. In the face of so much wretchedness I cannot stand the quaintness and safety of my mother-in-law's home any longer, and we are returning to Berlin.

MAY 1939

I believe this was our final good-bye. Ruth is on her way to Santiago de Chile. As children we swore to stay together forever. How difficult the separation was for both of us.

AUGUST 1939

Silvan and I went back to Frankfurt for another two weeks.

My mother had to leave Germany. She has gone to Brussels for now but wants to join my sister in Chile later on. Poor, beloved mother! How terribly hard the parting was and how bravely you bore it. But despite your fear and pain you still worried about me, the one who is safe. A wretched farewell at the train. I kissed your loving, caring hands one last time. I will never see you again.

Poor mother! I had to add a great sorrow to all of her disappointments and suffering. She could never understand my conversion to Christianity and accused me of having joined her enemies. It is true: people are evil and they hate us, but I had to follow my conscience. I am happy in my new faith. It brings joy to my life and gives me the strength to deal with my hardships. Christ is not our enemy and neither can a true Christian be. After all, Christ and his apostles, too, were Jews! And Mary, the most revered woman in the world, and St. Paul.

I have no mementos from my childhood home apart from a few photos of my loved ones. Whatever was not stolen had to be sold to pay for Ruth's expensive passage.

OCTOBER 1939

I am no longer safe in my home in Berlin. Because war has been on the horizon since the end of August, Gustav took our child and me to a women's cloister in Schlachtensee.[6] He feared that people in their war euphoria could beat us to death. The neighbors are very hateful, in particular the Nazi Women's League leader.[7] For some time now I have been afraid to walk home alone after dark. Will I be safe here?

NOVEMBER 1939

I am still in Schlachtensee. Gustav visits us every Saturday and stays until Monday morning. A few days ago we met a very fine Dominican priest;[8] he knows how to give us courage. Good "Uncle Erwin" has become little Silvan's favorite visitor.

NEW YEAR 1940

We are home again. We keep to ourselves and are content if no one does us harm. We could no longer stay in Schlachtensee. A lady who is a frequent guest there objected to living next door to a Jew. There was also a nun who told me that she felt very "German" and could no longer bear to look at me every day. She demanded that I be sent away. They did not even take pity on my child.

Father Erwin visits us often. He is the only one who still dares to set foot into our home. The neighbors stare and heckle him. He passes them with a smile on his lips and stands by us. He told me recently that the elderly lady in the flat below opened her door as he passed and looked him up and down. He politely stopped and asked her if he might be allowed to look her over as well. Furious, she slammed the door and will probably keep it shut in the future when he passes by. But I am afraid and expect more malice.

On Christmas, we played our instruments and sang together. Father Erwin played the flute and Gustav and I the piano. Together, we sang beautiful, traditional Christmas songs. Most were actually new to me. So, despite the troubled times we live in we had a few quiet and peaceful days. We want to sing together more often.

EASTER 1940 [MARCH 24, 1940]

I am finding the Triduum terribly hard to bear.[9] I almost collapse under the guilt that Judaism has to bear. "His blood shall be on us and on our children" [Matthew 27:25]. Is the current suffering of Jews an expiatory penalty for the murder of Christ? May others indict us or even judge us? Do they not murder Christ every day? Was it right that they burned down all synagogues here and across Germany?[10] How the sight of the burning houses of God horrified me! It is only now, in this time of despair, that I recognize how closely I am tied to my people. I will always stay true to them. The day after this heinous deed, as the ruins were still burning, Father Krawinkel, who has a difficult assignment in the heart of the city, came to see us to express his sorrow about this hooliganism.[11] I was consoled by the certainty that Christians do not approve of such "heroic deeds."

Jews disappear every day and no one knows what happens to them.[12] My cousin Herbert was taken to a camp near Leipzig. His dear old father told me that he received a letter informing him that Herbert had died in the camp. Did he wish to receive his ashes? Terrible things are happening! Now they have imprisoned his second and last son in a camp near Berlin. Paul is a decorated World War I veteran who fought bravely for Germany. For a long time, he volunteered in a field hospital specializing in highly infectious diseases. This is the gratitude he receives. Uncle Daniel is shockingly composed. He is a very mature and placid gentleman who quietly yields to his fate. Until the start of the war he owned several factories and houses but now he lives all alone in an attic room. It does not trouble him for his heart was never tied to earthly goods. But the anguish over his two sons has broken him.

AUGUST 1940

Silvan and I spent the summer in Upper Bavaria among good people free of hate. Silvan was cheerful and lively. He is a sweet and pious child. He pauses before every country shrine, and there are many in this region, and says: "*homo deus*, pray."[13] (We do not know where he learned this phrase; no one here admits to having taught him.) He folds his little hands and prays: "Dear God, so that I get into heaven, amen." That is all he can remember at this point. Content, he moves on until he comes across the next cross or shrine, where he repeats the scene. It is nearly impossible for me to sneak past any of them, not even once, because he takes my hand, drags me back, and says in an assertive tone of voice: "Mama, *homo deus*, pray." The child lives so naturally in the Christian faith.

Still, I was unable to find peace. Am I on the right path? Should I have abandoned Judaism in such trying times? It might have the appearance of abandonment but I tell everyone I come in contact with that I am of Jewish heritage. I am driven by the fear that people could think I am using my Christian faith to hide my Jewish roots. I owe this candor to Christendom as well as to my fellow Jews. Gustav and well-meaning priests warn me against this but I will never cease to be frank about it even though I am aware of placing myself in great danger.

Grim news from Brussels. The Germans have taken my brother. My mother, my sister-in-law, and twelve-year-old Heinz fled to the Dutch border where they encountered the war in all its terror.[14] In November 1939, mother finally received her ticket to South America but then war broke out and the steamer could no longer depart. How Ruth will worry about dear mother.

OCTOBER 1940

Now enemy airplanes are coming to Berlin more often.[15] Almost every night we are spending a few hours in the air-raid shelter. In the beginning I refused to go down there. I feared men more than bombs. Then I was forced to go down. My fears were justified. Despite the danger they are in, people cannot refrain from their nasty talk. When they notice that I am in the cellar with my boy but without my husband, they talk badly about Jews. Although I am in a separate cellar by myself (Jews are not allowed to be with Aryans), there is a broad corridor that connects both cellars and they know that I am forced to listen to their talk.[16] As an engineer, Gustav has been given the task to ensure people's safety in the air-raid shelter.[17] Everyone wants to be friends with him because they count on his help and feel secure in his presence. But he is very reticent and only does his duty. Still his concern for us both is touching and he spends every free minute at our side.

NOVEMBER 1940

When the tensions became unbearable, the Borromean sisters in the former seminary in Grünau graciously took in Silvan and me.[18] Will everything go well here? A better tone reigns in the air-raid shelter; we pray a lot. Nonetheless, I am restless. I do not like the people here. I had a conversation with a secondary school teacher who also lives here. She told me she was a devout Catholic. When I let her know that I, too, was a Catholic albeit of Jewish heritage, she freely admitted that she hated Jews. In response, I dared to point out to her that our savior, whom she worshipped, was also of Jewish blood. Outraged, she rejected my comment because Christ was God and therefore one could not make such a statement. Fine, I retorted, Christ is God but there is his mother, the greatest and holiest woman in the world who was a Jew and whom you too adore. Again an indignant reply: "No, Mary was a blonde Aryan." An educated woman uttered these words. Shaking my head, I went on my way and let her be. What is yet to come?

CHRISTMAS 1940

My distrust was justified. We were not allowed to celebrate Christmas with the others in the cloister. Several guests protested against having to spend Christmas with a Jew. Therefore, the sisters wanted to send us home. When they noticed my despair, they pointed us to our room and left us alone. Christmas, you feast of love and peace, where is your love, where is your conciliation?

JANUARY 1941

Over Christmas I made the acquaintance of Frau Herberg, a wonderful woman.[19] Her villa is right next to the house of the Borromean sisters and every day she attends Mass and takes Holy Communion. A true Christian who takes her faith seriously, she has already invited us to her home several times. She radiates great self-confidence and goodness, and I feel calm in her presence. Thus, despite the enmity we encountered here, we still experienced a few peaceful hours this Christmas.

FEBRUARY 1941

Because we encountered so much coldness in the convent we preferred to go back home. Now we once again sit in the air-raid shelter at night. Silvan and I share a cot. He is such a good boy. Usually I manage to carry him downstairs without waking him, and he sleeps until the all-clear signal is given. In case he wakes, I have a few puppets handy that tell him funny stories. That way he notices very little of this wretchedness, the noise of the antiaircraft guns and the thunder of the bombs, and I am not forced to listen to the negative talk around me.

Our home looks rather uncomfortable now. All windows are devoid of drapes and are covered only by blackout curtains. Water buckets and sand-filled boxes stand ready in the corners so that we can extinguish a fire. We did not darken the bedroom. When the sirens start howling, I instantly wake in terror and, in the darkness, I am unable to shake the horror that grips me. Mechanically, I reach for the outfits that are always laid out. Time is of the essence because soon the first bombs start falling. I quickly take Silvan wrapped in blankets into my arms while Gustav grasps the ever-ready air-raid-shelter suitcase. It is filled with some clothing, bread, and our most important documents. I rush to the cellar with the child. Gustav has to quickly open various doors, shut off the gas and water lines, and patrol the attic. He has to repeat this patrol several times over the course of the attack.

When we returned to our apartment after today's attack, we saw that an unexploded bomb had crashed through the ceiling into Silvan's bedroom. What luck that we were in the cellar.

MARCH 1941

Finally, news from my brother Max but it is terrible. He is in a concentration camp in the Eastern Pyrenees.[20] The letter reached us via the Swiss Red Cross. In Brussels, he was crammed into a cattle car and rode southward for days without receiving any food or being able to leave the car. Many died during the transport. In his despair he asked us to send him a towel, a pocketknife, and a bit of soap. His only shoes are worn out from long marches, his feet hurt in the hot sand, and his last belongings have been stolen. You are so sensitive and kind. How the misery in the camp must depress you.

I immediately turned to the Red Cross because I want to help but there is no way to send him anything from Germany. I will write to Uncle Emil in Zurich; if he is able to help he will.[21]

APRIL 1941

At the beginning of April, Silvan and I traveled to Frankfurt to visit my mother-in-law. She was very happy to see the boy again and spoiled him in grandmotherly fashion. The city, which I once loved above everything and where I spent a happy childhood, strikes me as unspeakably sad now that my mother and siblings have been driven from it. Since the desecration of the Jewish cemetery, I no longer have the courage to visit my father's grave.

For days I have begged my mother-in-law to go on holiday with us. She was reluctant but now she has promised to travel with us to her hometown of Bensheim.

Today, I wandered once again aimlessly and distraught through the city. When I came upon the first destroyed synagogues, I could not hold back my tears. I did not want to return home in this state of mind. Exhausted, I stepped inside the Capuchin cloister in the hope of finding a bit of solace there.[22] In response to my declaration that I was a convert, a brother asked me to have a seat in the waiting room. When the door reopened, an elderly priest with a long white beard stood before me. The sight startled me and I stuttered that I was struggling with my faith, which was the truth. But such a thing did not figure in this priest's world. Probably no one had ever admitted this to him so openly. After shouting at me, he abruptly showed me the door. This encounter was terribly distressing for me. If only Father Erwin were nearby. He would understand that one can become confused in this terrible time.

I am myself once again. I am spending a few peaceful days in the St. Mary's Institute of the Loreto Sisters in Bensheim, where my mother-in-law was educated many years ago.[23] As a former student, she was welcomed most warmly, and so were we. A few older teachers remembered her. The quiet here soothes me. I have already spoken with the institute's priest, a very gracious and understanding gentleman. He likes Jews and respects them!

GOOD FRIDAY 1941

Silvan is sad about the evil men whose fault it is that Christ has to lie on the ground. He wants to be good, so He [Christ] can once again go on top of the altar.[24]

EASTER 1941 [APRIL 13]

Peace has once again returned to my heart. Yesterday, I went to confession and today I received Holy Communion. Responding to my urgings, my mother-in-law turned back to her faith and she too received the holy sacraments. As a result, we have become closer.

I took a bit of vengeance on the Capuchins. My nasty impression of them remains with me, and whenever I see a bearded priest from the nearby cloister walk through the village, I remember my experience in Frankfurt. When Silvan refused to eat at table, I said to him: "If you don't behave and empty your plate then a Capuchin monk with a long beard will come by and put you in a sack." He looked at me and laughed because he did not believe such a thing was possible. To threaten him, I took him by the hand and led him outside. Oh, my, as if I had ordered it, immediately two Capuchin brothers with long beards came down the street. As soon as Silvan saw them, he began to wail so terribly that the two alarmed gentlemen started to walk toward us to inquire what was wrong with the child. They could not know that their long beards were the cause of the howling; they looked benevolent and friendly.

The boy, who usually fears no one, was to have one more frightening encounter with a Capuchin. A Catholic sister, whom I told about my experience in Frankfurt, sought to improve my opinion of the Capuchins, and she proposed to take me to a priest with whom she was acquainted. We took Silvan along. An old friendly brother with a toothless mouth opened the gate. But Silvan only saw the long white beard and started to howl again. When the good brother saw the horrified face of the child, he started to laugh so heartily that the boy calmed down immediately and even gave him a hearty handshake. The two of them have since become good friends. The friendly Capuchin taught me that I must not paint everyone with the same brush. He was not only very kind but he also understood the challenges of our age. I am once again at peace.

MAY 1941

We are back in Berlin. Gustav is glad to have us back again. His work in the laboratory no longer gratifies him. He is a good scientist who is needed but he nonetheless feels vulnerable among his Nazi colleagues since it is common knowledge that he is married to a Jew. A few days ago, at the request of his plant manager, he had to give a talk at the Technical College.[25] He feared that anyone in the audience could interrupt his presentation and forbid him to continue because as a race defiler he is not permitted to speak publicly. Luckily, everything went well.

On the other hand, he had yet another clash with our local party leader, whom I do not know personally. This man told Gustav that he considers it a provocation merely to have to see me.

JUNE 1941

Gustav took his vacation early this year since one never knows if things are going to get worse and I will not be allowed to travel at all anymore. Even now it is quite difficult. Following the advice of Father Erwin, we traveled by way of Innsbruck to Fulpmes. But the family he recommended we stay with had no room for us. We could not take rooms in a guesthouse because I have to register with the name "Sara" that was forced upon me and that would unmask me as a Jew.[26] We had already been on the road for twenty-four hours and were dead tired when we dared to approach the local priest, Father Dr. Telzer, a good and wise old gentleman.[27] He gave us a letter of recommendation and directed us to a farmer in Pettnau. As he was writing, our son, Silvan, exhausted, laid down under the desk on the carpet like a little dog and fell asleep. The old priest was touched. He promised to help and organized accommodations for us for the night. The next morning, we took the train to Oberinntal and against our expectations, we are spending a few lovely days in Pettnau. Gustav was pretty discouraged, and the peace and quiet here are calming him.

CORPUS CHRISTI 1941 [THURSDAY, JUNE 12, 1941]

Today I experienced great joy. A week ago I had a conversation with the two little girls of the innkeeper. We talked about the Corpus Christi celebrations, and I asked them if they planned to scatter flowers before the Blessed Sacrament, a custom I knew from my time in Frankfurt. They were wholly unfamiliar with this practice but after I told them about it, they became quite excited and wanted me to ask the local priest for permission to introduce this tradition here as well. They planned on persuading several other children to join them. I did them the favor and talked with the local priest. He was very skeptical, though, since the farmers were unfamiliar with the tradition and quite conservative besides. He finally gave in, provided that at least four girls had parental permission to participate, something he doubted very much. He also mentioned that this year the procession was to take place without music or singing because all the young lads had been conscripted. On Friday I went from farmhouse to farmhouse and spoke with parents about my plan, and on Saturday fourteen girls came forward. First, I practiced a few hymns with them so that our singing might add to the feast. I also ordered a flower basket for each child. Each girl had a white dress, and most also had a wreath to adorn their hair. For those who did not, we quickly crafted one. Yesterday the girls went with me to the blooming meadows where we collected a large hamper full of lovely flowers so that I could fill each girl's basket.

Today everything went splendidly. The girls sang with me during the entire procession and at all four altars. They did well, and the farmers were elated. But happiest of all was little Silvan. Dressed in a pretty black velvet suit amid the white-clad girls, he resembled the little Christ child, as he too strewed flowers before the dear Redeemer. The local priest thanked me later for my troubles. He praised me and remarked that I, as a lay person, could risk engaging the children in religious activities whereas he had to fear the party. Then and there I was gripped by a terrible rage. I told him that I was a Jew, and that I did not even have the right to speak to an Aryan child. Stunned, he remained silent. The stakes are high and I must not succumb to hate. I hope I did not harm myself too much with my frankness. I have to think of Gustav and Silvan; they both need to recuperate.

LATE JUNE 1941

I am constantly surrounded by children and hardly have time for myself anymore. We sing old German folk songs and dance lovely folk dances that I remember from my schooldays. The children are amenable and I take great joy in teaching them. They even come in the evening when I am very tired, and then I have to go to the meadows with them, to sing and dance. Usually little Silvan enthusiastically tags along but Gustav grows quite jealous of the many children who steal me away time and again. Is it not strange that I of all people, a Jew, a racial alien, teach these children German songs and German dances? (Despite my ostracization, I very much love my native country and feel that I am a German.) Gustav returned to Berlin. He wants us to stay here as long as possible.

JULY 15, 1941

Today I received the holy sacrament of Confirmation from Bishop Paulus of Innsbruck.[28] I first attended Mass in his private chapel and afterward I was confirmed. Monsignor Weiskopf was my sponsor.[29] He has been my confessor for some time now. He and Professor Schmid, whom I often visited on the Stichlberg, prepared me for this day with much devotion and understanding.

LATE AUGUST 1941

We are back in Berlin. The atmosphere here is becoming increasingly perilous. When someone dares to speak to me in the street, he immediately receives a warning from the local party leader along with the threat that if it should happen again the "crime" would be made public in the SS newspaper *Der Stürmer*.[30]

Only recently Frau L., the wife of a pharmacist, spoke to me. Her boy is the same age as Silvan. We got on well, and she expressed the wish to become my friend. I told her that, unfortunately, it was impossible because I was a Jew. She replied that this fact made absolutely no difference to her and nothing could prevent her from standing by me, especially since I was a fellow Catholic. I had to smile when I told her that three days from now she would no longer even greet me in the street. And that is what happened. Someone threatened to report her to the Gestapo. When she accidentally runs into me now, she looks the other way. I know the steadfastness of mankind.

They will not even leave my small child in peace. For a few minutes I left him outside of a shop in which I had to buy something, when older boys from our street, egged on by their parents, threw bricks at Silvan. Luckily, they did not injure him seriously. A few days before, I left him alone in front of our house for a short time. He went over to a few children to shake hands with them, but they ran away and shouted that they were not allowed to play with him because he had a contagious disease. Horrified, Silvan ran over to me to tell me that he was not sick. He could not comprehend what was happening.

He does, however, understand that the lady who lives beneath us is evil. He recently took down his "old witch" puppet that hangs above his little bed next to Hansel and Gretel. He brought her into the kitchen, washed her under the faucet and quickly put her into the oven. Turning toward me he said: "First we wash her so that the blood comes out and now we make a good roast out of the old witch." He probably thought about the old witch in the fairy tale but I soon noticed that he identified her with the wicked old woman in our house. I was quite shaken by his game and had to tell him that the lady was indeed old but not evil. I told him this even though I knew better and perhaps for this reason he remained skeptical. He probably wanted to wash out the blood because he saw me do it once with a chicken. How careful one must be around children.

I am visiting my cousin Grete Merzbach more often.[31] She is half Aryan and a Protestant like her father. But because she is married to a Jew, both she and her little daughter are considered full Jews.[32] Little Ute is six years old now. She is a pretty, darling child, assiduously and attentively raised. But first and foremost she is very smart, which does not surprise me since both of her parents have earned doctorates with high distinction. I feel at ease in their cultured home. In addition to Greek and Latin, Grete also taught religion at a high school for girls, and she helps me overcome my spiritual conflicts. She has long since been dismissed from her post at the school but she was granted permission to teach her child along with other Jewish girls privately.

OCTOBER 1941

For a while I was a member of the church choir in our little parish. Singing has always given me much joy, but now I had to give it up because a few singers did not like the idea of a Jew participating. I always remained modestly, even shyly, in the background. Still, I am not wanted.

NOVEMBER 1941

These gloomy, foggy days depress me terribly. I cannot shake my feelings of perpetual fear and restlessness. What is yet to come! I miss Father Erwin very much. Lately he has visited us often. His even temper and cheerfulness and most of all his deep religiosity have had a positive influence on me. He is currently staying in a small town in Westphalia, where he is painting a church, and he will not return until after Christmas. Will I be able to cope without him?

LATE DECEMBER 1941

I spent Christmas in the church of the Oratorians.[33] Father Krawinkel, who sensed my desolation, invited us over on the afternoon of St. Stephen's Day, and we spent a few peaceful hours there.[34] He showed much empathy for the plight of Jews, and he senses how much I suffer from the violent anti-Jewish measures. He invited me to participate in a discussion group of young women academics who meet once a week under his guidance.

JANUARY 1942

Silvan and I frequently visit Frau Herberg in Grünau. I often try to resolve religious issues with her. She is so calm and confident; her faith is unshakable. Nothing unsettles her, whereas I am commonly led astray by people.

FEBRUARY 1942

Father L., the confessor of Frau Herberg whom I sometimes visit, spoke to me.[35] He is worried about the family and fears that my visits could harm them. I understand his concerns but I was still very hurt because he said that in Germany I was like a leper and like them, I, too, must take care that people do not come near me. Hard words. From now on I will of course refrain from inconveniencing the Herberg family.

I visited the religious workshop in the Francis Xavier Home.[36] Father K[rawinkel] first read from the letters of St. Paul. Afterward there was a general exchange. My heart was not really in it, and I did not dare to share my difficulties with the others. Father K. sensed this. Afterward, he called me over and invited me to ask him questions. He understood that I could not talk publicly about my problems, which hail from my Jewish upbringing. Because it was late and he worried about my safety, he accompanied me home. The Francis Xavier Home is located in the bleakest inner city where in narrow, dirty, and seedy lanes much nastiness and crimes of the worst sort are at home. But the home, which is primarily intended for female university students, is an oasis of spiritual cleanliness and propriety. Even though we live in a "respectable" area, where many civil-servant families live very honorably, they nonetheless believe that as good National Socialists they must not leave the Jew in peace. Their hate knows no bounds. When these people find that it is permissible to shed their good manners, they probably become more dangerous than the underworld near the Alexanderplatz.[37]

LATE FEBRUARY 1942

Frau Herberg came to see me to inquire why I have not come to see her. I told her of my conversation with Father L. but she would hear none of it. She consciously stands by me and insists that I continue to come and visit her. This once again gives me courage and the certainty that Christianity lived makes people strong and good. It convinces me that I must remain steadfast in my new faith but I will nonetheless curtail my visits.

MARCH 1942

Lately the Gestapo has conducted several searches of our home but they did not find anything "suspicious." I probably have to burn my extensive correspondence with Catholic priests. Among others, Bishop Paulus from Innsbruck has written to me occasionally, and even though all of these letters are of a purely pastoral nature, the very act of writing to a Jew incriminates these gentlemen. Luckily, they have not yet found the folder containing my correspondence. I will destroy the letters, no matter how dear they are to me.

The Gestapo seized our radio.[38] At first Gustav was inconsolable because in the evening he liked to listen to a good organ or piano concert for relaxation. He does see, however, that it is probably better if we do not have a radio anymore even though we never dared (our walls have ears) to listen to foreign broadcasts.[39] It would surely have occurred to our dear neighbors soon enough to report us for it.

APRIL 1942

All Jews must now wear the Jewish star, a black Star of David against a yellow background.[40] Because Gustav is Aryan I am exempt from this

decree. It would have been a terrible burden for me because Jews are
no longer allowed to use trains, neither city trains nor the subway, neither electric trams nor coach buses.[41] Considering the sprawl that is
Berlin, this is a significant prohibition. I hardly can venture outside in
my neighborhood anymore because people will not leave me in peace.
For the same reason, I can also no longer go to the local church in our
suburb. I therefore travel every morning to St. Hedwig Cathedral
where Father Erwin celebrates Mass daily at 10:00 a.m. Afterward he
goes for a walk with Silvan and me in the Tiergarten, where I can speak
with him about my difficulties with my faith. (He is the only one who
still dares to show himself in public with us.) He tries to cheer me up
whenever he can. He goes on boat rides with us and rides the carousel
with Silvan. He does everything in his power to bring some joy into
our lives.

Nurse Jutta, a pious Protestant convert, told me that a fellow nurse
was incensed about the fact that in the Dominican church a man wearing
the yellow star dared to approach the communion rail.[42] In the nurse's
mind, he did much damage to the Christian community and perhaps
chased a number of good Germans away from the communion rail. Sister
Jutta was as outraged as I about this point of view. Now something similar happened in our parish church. A Jewish convert, who has to wear
the Jewish star, was asked to think of the other parishioners, and, if
he had to attend Mass, at the very least take a seat in the choir loft.
Because he is such a deeply pious man, he now takes a seat in the choir
loft where no one can see him.[43]

EARLY MAY 1942

In a few days Gustav starts his vacation. We have no idea where to go. He
really needs a holiday because he is so worn out from work. But he is
afraid of traveling because with me by his side he will not find accommodations anywhere. I suggested that he go on his own but he will not
hear of it. Then we received news that his mother was sick, so for now he
will travel to Frankfurt. Because it is too dangerous for the child and me
to remain in Berlin on our own, we will first travel to Innsbruck to consult with my confirmation sponsor to see if he knows anyone who will
take us in for a few weeks.

LATE MAY 1942

We have been spending a lovely holiday on an old farmstead about two hours from Brixlegg. My confirmation sponsor was out of town when I arrived in Innsbruck at the beginning of May, and not knowing what to do, I randomly traveled to the Unterinntal. I disembarked in Brixlegg and, seeking to avoid the many tourists there, I hiked up the mountain to the small village of Reith. Upon arrival, I turned for help to the local priest,[44] who told his parochial vicar to accompany us. We visited several very isolated farms because the kind priest was of the opinion that people who lived in such solitude would be more generous and willing to assist.[45] A few of the farmers would indeed have helped me, but everyone with a spare room had already taken in lodgers. We finally found a room on a large farmstead. We feel secure here in this glorious isolation. Gustav, to whom I sent a message via telegraph, has since joined us. His mother is improving, and he likes it here as well.

JUNE 1942

Gustav's vacation is over and he has returned to Berlin. We, on the other hand, will stay for as long as possible in our safe little corner of the world. Unfortunately, Silvan and I must leave here in a few days because our room is needed. The parochial vicar from Reith offered to help us find new accommodations, and so we went on a long hike to several remote farmsteads high up in the mountains. I can actually take four-year-old Silvan on these long hikes. He enjoys walking and does not tire easily. The farmers were all very friendly and open-minded but, without exception, all of them had many children and little room. Everyone was most hospitable, compelling us to help ourselves to food and drink. One farmstead, remote and high up, will take us in for a while. There is little room but they will move closer together to make space.

LATE JULY 1942

We have been up here on the mountain farmstead near Brixlegg for six weeks already. The people are nice. Now the pastor in Brixlegg has informed me that the Gestapo has learned of my presence and is searching for me. I was advised to leave. Even in this isolated spot they have found me. I had forgotten that my hosts had to register me with the police in Brixlegg, and even though I wrote my Jewish maiden name as illegibly as possible on the form, it must nonetheless have raised suspicion.[46]

AUGUST 1942

We had to leave the lovely Unterinntal in a hurry. I was too tired to search for new accommodations for my boy and me in Tyrol and so we returned to Berlin.

At home I found a letter from Uncle Emil. He sent my brother the requested items along with a number of other things and money. Max thanked him. Apparently, he is doing very poorly. Uncle Emil wants to keep helping him. I am very grateful to him because I worry so much about my poor brother, and I cannot help him.

Gustav, who, as the air-raid warden, has been in possession of a gas mask for some time, was worried that Silvan and I would be without protection in case of an emergency. The NSV [National Socialist People's Welfare] now sells gas masks to anyone with the means to pay and also fits the masks to each person upon purchase.[47] Gustav took us there but, suspecting problems, he left us outside of the office and went in alone. In response to his request, the official of the NSV told him that gas masks were quite pointless for Jews. Gustav really wanted to knock this man to the ground but he stopped himself out of consideration for us and exited the room in silence. Outside, he was almost overcome by a fit of rage. My poor dear companion, you suffer even more than I do from this inhumane behavior.

For some time now Jews have been allowed to shop only between the hours of 4:00 and 5:00 in the afternoon, and they cannot purchase fruits or vegetables anymore.[48] I am also no longer permitted to pick up our ration coupons from the ration office. A separate office for Jews has been opened at the Adlershof, and Jews' coupons are marked with a large "J."[49] They get neither meat nor sugar nor white bread.[50] I get regular coupons for Gustav and Silvan.

The shops do not sell fruit and vegetables to me, which is neither here nor there because in the afternoon, when I am allowed to set foot inside the shops, there is nothing left in any case. Gustav has to get these things on his way home from work because working people with a special pass can have items held for them. It weighs heavily on me that he has to take care of these things when he is so tired and stressed. He never used to accompany us to the store voluntarily; he found it unmanly. He has now forced himself to take on this task as an act of charity and love toward me. He really is a fine companion.

Since Silvan needs milk in the morning, the little one has to get it himself. I go with him as far as I can but I cannot go inside the shop and have to send him in alone. The other women have started to mercilessly gossip that the Jewish woman sends her child shopping at a time when it is forbidden for her. Now they do not want to serve the little one anymore. How cruel people are. Even mothers refuse to share my distress. How must those Jews fare who are marked with the yellow star? Whenever I want to escape, I go to a different part of the city where no one knows me. And when no one takes offense at my somewhat foreign appearance, my dark hair and my black eyes, I can even shop whenever I want. But I am never at ease when I do this. What if an acquaintance recognizes me as I am breaking the law?

There are no longer many Jews out and about. Many have been deported. No one knows where they have been taken.

LATE SEPTEMBER 1942

I traveled with Gustav to Frankfurt to visit his gravely ill mother. We took Silvan to Frau Herberg where he was well cared for. Even though there was no hope of my mother-in-law's recovery we had to leave. Gustav could not stay away for long from his laboratory because he has begun a series of important experiments, and I worried so much about our boy that I, too, did not give in to my mother-in-law's pleading that we stay. Now that I see how well Silvan is doing, I severely reproach myself for my heartlessness. Before I said my farewells, I arranged for the local priest to pay her a visit. After not going to confession for a long time, she finally confessed, and the priest promised me that he would in good time administer the last rites. I also tried to hire a Catholic nurse, and I even approached the Franciscan sisters but they had no one available for in-home care. They advised me to move mother to the Catholic hospital but she refused to leave her home. I was forced to hire a civilian nurse who did not make a good impression on me. N.S.[51]

OCTOBER 1942

We were back in Berlin for just fourteen days when a telegram sum-
moned us back to Frankfurt. Unfortunately, Gustav's mother passed
away before he arrived. My misgivings about the unsuited nurse were
justified. A good longtime friend of my mother-in-law told me that
the nurse was quite unkind. She also neglected to call for the priest in
time, so that my mother-in-law did not receive the last rites. I once
again reproach myself that I did not stay with her until the end. We
solemnly laid her to rest and had a Requiem Mass said in the parish
church.

LATE OCTOBER 1942

Father Erwin also said a solemn Requiem Mass in St. Hedwig Cathedral
that we all attended. Gustav took the death of his dear mother very hard.
Now there is one less person in this hostile world who stands by him. He
has had no contact with his other relatives for quite a while. He has sev-
ered all ties because they do not want anything to do with me. Gustav
now lives entirely for me and our child.

NOVEMBER 1942

I went to see Dr. Merzbach and family. They had to give up their lovely
home and now live in a small and dreary furnished room.[52] Grete lacks
even the most basic foods for Uta. More and more items have been crossed
off the ration cards for Jews. Even for her child she receives neither sugar
nor flour and, of course, no fruits or vegetables. But she does not complain
and bravely bears her difficult lot. Her husband directs the deportation of
the Jewish population, and so he is traveling most of the time, to
Litzmannstadt or Theresienstadt, where, it is said, most of the Jews are
being taken.[53] So she lives alone and in fear that they will take her and her
child away as well. Even though her father was a well-known official in the
Aviation Ministry, no one can help her.

LATE DECEMBER 1942

We had a bleak Christmas. I lack all inner peace. Life is so mercilessly
hard, the horror of what is happening so great. Where is God? If He does

not reveal Himself in the love and kindness of mankind where else can I find Him? We are surrounded by nothing but hate and destruction. Father Erwin tells us that the Jews are all being carted off. Large camps have been set up in Litzmannstadt and Theresienstadt where they are to be settled. But there is no news about what goes on there. Do they leave the poor, persecuted people there in peace at last?

JANUARY 1943

Both of us play a lot of music these days. When I am seized by despair during the day, I sit and play the piano. It is my greatest joy when little Silvan sits next to me and with a serious expression listens to the lovely old folk melodies. And how heartily he can laugh when I play a funny children's tune.

In the evening, Gustav also seeks respite at the piano. I sit quietly next to him and dream about a different, peaceful world, where I, too, am a human being of equal worth. Beethoven, Bach, Brahms, and Mozart are our friends. All the evil that surrounds us slips away until late in the evening when the air-raid sirens wrest us from our dreams. Then we find ourselves once again returned to the merciless, grim reality in which the horror of war engulfs us and people pounce on us like beasts with their evil talk.

FEBRUARY 1943

I have to keep telling myself: Amid the malice and meanness that I see, I must not forget the magnanimous and generous human beings that still exist even here. But the many acts of cruelty and humiliation threaten to gradually suffocate me. In our street there is a black bulletin board belonging to the party, where *Der Stürmer*, this greatest of tabloid rags, is often displayed.[54] Many people pause before it and take in the pictures. During the past few days, there was once again a display of Jewish "caricatures" with devilish grimaces in which all kinds of base instincts were evoked. I almost could not resist the temptation to stand next to it and call out to the passersby: "See here, I, too, am a Jewish subhuman!" I know that I look respectable and that my face bears no resemblance to these grotesque faces.

MARCH 1, 1943

When Silvan and I as usual went to St. Hedwig Cathedral this morning, we did not notice until we stood directly before it that it had burned down to its foundations.[55] It had become a victim of the previous night's air raid. Even my child was so struck by the gruesome sight of devastation that he repeatedly called out: "Oh, the beautiful church. Where will Father Erwin now celebrate Mass?" But when we learned that a priest had risked his life to rescue the Blessed Sacrament from the church the boy cheered up because at least God was taken out of the burning church.[56]

MARCH 6, 1943

For weeks I have been living in fear of having my child torn from me as I am deported to one of the infamous camps. Nonetheless, I was completely caught off guard when I answered the door yesterday afternoon and a man, accompanied by an SS soldier with a rifle, identified himself as a member of the Gestapo and demanded entry. When I hesitated, they roughly pushed me aside and forced their way inside the apartment. He told me I had to come along immediately and that I should pack a few necessities, since one never knew if I would ever return. As soon as he heard these words my little boy started to wail terribly, whereupon they took him to my neighbor, a teacher loyal to the party. Then they loaded me onto a truck where several people were already cowering in despair. My plea for permission to quickly phone Gustav fell on deaf ears. We crisscrossed Berlin and stopped from time to time to pick up more unfortunate people. I was in agony because I did not know how Silvan was faring, and the screams of my child when they took him from me still echoed in my ears. Incapable of taking any interest in my surroundings, I apathetically sat in a corner of the truck.[57]

We were unloaded at the central collection point for Jews in the Grosse Hamburger Strasse, and along with the others, I was pushed into a small room already filled with many people.[58] Some of them lay on the floor, men, women, and children. Confronted with this wretchedness, I was gripped by a deep despair and made my way to the door so that I could leave. From all sides people implored me to do nothing hasty that might result in immediate deportation to Litzmannstadt. But detention drove me nearly mad and besides, I had to try to get back to my child since I believed him to be in danger. I aimlessly wandered through the now deserted hallways and finally came upon an office. How I managed to find compassion there I do not know. I talked about my worry for my child. I had to wait outside of the office for several hours. Finally, they took down my personal information, including the fact that my husband was Aryan. Then they asked for my papers but in all of the excitement I had forgotten to take even a single document. Apparently, this made the whole affair more difficult. I once again had to wait for a long time, left in the dark about my fate. In the end, they seemed to believe my answers even without documentation and gave me written authorization to leave. It was now almost midnight, and after the anxious wait and the fear of what might come, my nerves were strained to a breaking point. I could barely make it through the remainder of the ordeal. I had to pass an entire column of SS soldiers with my permit, and several checked it meticulously. At last, I received my final stamp and was allowed to pass through the main gate.[59] I was barely outside when gunfire erupted nearby. The shots were surely not aimed at me but it put my already shattered nerves into such a state, I was incapable of going home on my own. On top of it, I was physically exhausted because I had not eaten anything all day. I knew of a Catholic hospital near the camp.[60] I soon found it and went up to the gate, where I asked to speak to the mother superior but I was told that she had retired for the night.[61] I then asked for and was directed to the resident chaplain.[62] I gathered what little strength I had left and told the priest what had happened. I asked for his protection. Although I was clearly quite shaken by the horror of the experience, he did not believe a word of what I told him and said I could be a spy. Considering my state of fear and anxiety, I cannot believe that I could have given him that impression. He denied my request to phone Father Erwin, who, I hoped, would pick me up from there and take me home, on the grounds that the priest would hardly be willing to do this. It was then that I thought of Frau Herberg as a way out of this situation since I could not reach Gustav via telephone. The priest finally connected me with Frau Herberg, who had already heard of the day's events. She was so happy about my regained freedom that she wanted to meet me halfway. The priest seemed to trust me a little bit more now and sent someone to accompany me to the train. We had to pass by the transit camp again and were once more caught in a shoot-out. We sought shelter in an entryway but after a while we continued on our way to the train undisturbed.

Gustav was completely unnerved by fear for me, and he cried uncontrollably when he saw me. In the afternoon, he had found the note that I was permitted to write under the supervision of the Gestapo official. Once he read the message about my arrest, he immediately contacted Father Erwin. Then he went to the police to inquire where I had been taken. The police had no information and sent him to the Gestapo, where he was told he was just going to have to wait until he was notified.

Silvan was still with the teacher. Frau Herberg wanted to pick him up but the teacher brought him to me herself. She told me how much she had enjoyed my charming child and how glad she was that I had returned. Her kind act of taking in my child reconciles me with many things. I did not expect this. Silvan is quite gregarious and has conquered this woman's heart. She no longer harbors any hate toward me and was most helpful.

Father Erwin came very early this morning to inquire after Silvan's whereabouts and news about me. When I opened the door, he was quite speechless with joy. He had prayed a lot for me. I told him about the distrust I encountered, and he assured me that without question, he would have taken me home. I never doubted for even one moment his readiness to help us.

LATE MARCH 1943

I was supposed to pick up my ration cards a few days after my release from the camp, but since I was still utterly exhausted from my ordeal, Gustav volunteered for the task. What a stroke of luck! All Jews who went to the distribution office, even those who had been released from the camp in the Grosse Hamburger Strasse, were once again arrested.[63] But they could not do anything to Gustav. He said I was sick. In the afternoon, a Gestapo agent came again to our home. I was in bed at the time, and I heard through the door that the Gestapo was there. They went from room to room, and when they passed the door to the bathroom for a second time, I heard them say: "What a lovely home you have!" I was gripped by a terrible fear that they would arrest me again. A while later, as I realized that the man was leaving, relief washed over me. Gustav told me that the agent interrogated him in detail about his political convictions. He replied truthfully that he had never belonged to a political party but that he was a good German. Why then did he have a Jewish wife? Well, because he loved me. Then the agent asked him, "But what is the child doing here?" As anger welled up inside of him, Gustav was unable to reply. They consider our lovely and good child a subhuman.

Every time Father Erwin came by for a visit, he frightened me terribly when he rang the doorbell since I live in constant fear of being taken away. To spare me the terror, he now knocks when he comes. Not long ago Silvan frightened me in an overcrowded tram when he asked loudly: "Mama, when will the Gestapo come for you again?"

I tried to visit Grete a few days ago. She no longer lives in her room. She, too, was taken to the Grosse Hamburger Strasse where she and her child have been held for the past three weeks. Because it is merely a transit camp, she will migrate from there to one of the infamous other camps. Poor Grete![64]

EARLY APRIL 1943

At the end of March I received a summons to the employment office for Jews. Now that Silvan has turned five, I am obligated to work. This would not have been so bad in and of itself but because Aryans cannot be expected to work alongside a Jew, I was nearly taken to a labor camp.[65] But once again God held His protective hand over me. Even though it was prohibited, Gustav accompanied me to the employment office, and he never left my side. He did not let them berate him when he joined me and other Jews in the queue. One official in particular made quite a scene, screaming at my husband: "Are you aware that you are married to a full-blooded Jew?" Yet he immediately ordered me to go back home. I have the feeling that the official wanted to help me but to make sure it did not attract attention he adopted a very rough tone toward me. I assume they will leave me alone for the time being.

Erna Becker-Kohen in 1980.
Courtesy of Esther-Maria Nägele.

Erna Becker-Kohen in 1934.
Courtesy of Esther-Maria Nägele.

Gustav Becker. Courtesy of Esther-Maria Nägele.

Gustav, Erna, and Silvan Becker in 1939. Courtesy of Esther-Maria Nägele.

Isabella Kohen, Erna, and Silvan Becker in 1939. Courtesy of Esther-Maria Nägele.

Isabella Kohen. Courtesy of
Esther-Maria Nägele.

Erna and Silvan Becker, Christmas in Berlin, 1939. Courtesy of Esther-Maria Nägele.

Maria Herberg. Courtesy of
Esther-Maria Nägele.

Sefa Lochbihler. Courtesy of
Esther-Maria Nägele.

Michl Lochbihler. Courtesy of
Esther-Maria Nägele.

Father Erwin Röhr (far left) in Imberg in June 1944. Courtesy of Esther-Maria Nägele.

Maria Ladner and her children in Pettnau in April 1945. Courtesy of Esther-Maria Nägele.

Father Paul Anton Sinz.
Courtesy of Esther-Maria Nägele.

Silvan and Erna Becker in
Mehrerau. Courtesy of
Esther-Maria Nägele.

Silvan Becker with his
parents on his First Holy
Communion day in 1948.
Courtesy of Esther-Maria
Nägele.

APRIL 15, 1943

Yesterday, I received news from Brussels that my dear good mother had died in the local hospital there on April 11. Even though the worry about my only brother, who was deported in 1940, killed her, at least she still died a natural death.[66] Poor mother! None of your children could be with you! In the hour of your death, did you forgive me for converting to Christianity?

Today, Father Erwin said a Requiem Mass for my dear mother in the vestry of the former St. Hedwig Cathedral. The vestry has been converted into a temporary chapel. Saying a silent Mass was all he could do for this woman of a different faith. Dear mother, I know for sure that you are in a good place. Your life was nothing but worry and toil for your children. But despite the countless worries for your own family that you took on after our father died so young, you always had a good heart and an open hand for every poor and troubled person you met.

LATE APRIL 1943

Father Erwin told me that unless they were deported to a different camp, most of the Jews that were arrested with me were released after several weeks. Others like Grete and Uta are still there. A few were released after only fourteen days. Dear God, I thank you for your intervention. I could not have borne this unjust imprisonment for very long. The experiences of that day still weigh heavily on me, and I am unable to put them behind me. When I am alone, I am often overcome by a terrible fear. I think being confined is the worst thing in the world.

MAY 1943

When I shared with Father Erwin how sorry I was that I had lost my St. Benedict medal a while back,[67] he told me that a Benedictine priest from Ettal was preaching the following Sunday afternoon in Erkner.[68] He encouraged me to go and afterward ask the priest for a medal. After some hesitation, I decided to go and thus I made the acquaintance of a very wise and kind priest. Perhaps prompted by my shyness, he asked me if there was something else I wished to tell him. In response, I shared my troubles with him. I spoke about being cast out and my spiritual conflicts.

He showed much empathy for my situation, and sincerely shared my sense of being hounded. He promised over and over to help me as much as possible through deeds but especially through prayer. I felt very safe in his presence until I noticed that it was getting dark, and I became terrified of making my way home. For some time now I have not ventured outside after dark because I fear other people. Father Lukas sensed my anxiety and said he would accompany me home.[69] In the darkened, overcrowded tram it was good to know a familiar person nearby. At home, Father Lukas also met Gustav and Silvan, and he promised to write to us; he said he would not forget us.

I received another summons to the employment office. I am earmarked for forced labor but since Gustav works for a company central to the war effort and I have to care for my child, I was granted another deferment, but for how long?

LATE MAY 1943

I received a lovely letter from Father Lukas, whose acquaintance I had made in Erkner. He writes that he is looking for a place for Silvan and me somewhere in the south of Germany. Yes, I would rather go south. People are warmer and kinder there. Berlin never felt like home to me. This giant city with its cold industriousness devoid of any tradition always roused feelings of fear and forlornness in me. Though I love my home, even its immediate environs are foreign to me. Ever since my detention in the Grosse Hamburger Strasse, I can't shake my feelings of insecurity. I live in constant fear of a catastrophe. What is yet to come? Separation from my family and deportation to Theresienstadt? I would prefer to be beaten to death right here and now since I cannot bear being separated from my loved ones for very long. The most frightening question: What will become of Silvan? Father Erwin is very worried about us. I do not think he expects any good news. For a while now measures against Jews have been stepped up again.

JUNE 15, 1943, 2:00 P.M.

In one hour we must leave our home. This morning an agitated Father Erwin came by to tell me that I had to leave Berlin this very day because tomorrow I will no longer have the opportunity.[70] Starting tomorrow, in order to control the evacuees (Dr. Goebbels's call to evacuate Berlin has caused an atmosphere of panic in the city), the NSV is taking charge of the distribution of all rail tickets. Of course, Jews will not receive any tickets from this organization. I immediately called Gustav at the laboratory and asked him to come home. He decided to take his furlough right away so that he could take us to safety. Gustav returned to work to ask his director to grant him leave, and, with Father Erwin's assistance, I packed the most necessary items: A few suitcases with clothing, a large wicker trunk with linens. As usual, Father Erwin was most helpful. Wait! Photos, reminders of peaceful days and of home and family, were quickly torn from albums. (Those would have been too heavy to take.) I took the picture of mother from the frame that sits atop the desk, and I threw everything into one of the already full suitcases. Take the valuable jewelry! I may need it on my journey.

Now I must say farewell to these familiar spaces, to the room in which Silvan came into this world. For the last time, I gaze out the window. The handsome street and, across from it, the dark deciduous woods seem so peaceful. How beautifully situated our home is! I only realize it now in the moment I have to leave it. Forever? Dear Lord, what is yet to come? We journey into the unknown. Father Lukas, whom I called a few days ago in Ettal, has promised to look for a place for us. Now there is no time to wait for his message. Today, we can only travel as far as Frankfurt an der Oder but we must take care to journey on from there as quickly as possible.

AUGUST 1943

Thank God! We have finally found a quiet place. We are in Tannheim in a remote corner of Tyrol, near the Oberjochpass, now called Adolf-Hitler-Pass, which leads into the Allgäu. Old Mother Binosa has taken us in with much kindness.[71] I immediately trusted this pious old woman. I told her that I am on the run and that the Gestapo will eventually search for me. Frau Binosa is most eager to help and suggested that I speak to her son Siegfried,[72] the proprietor of the Adler pub, since I could trust him and he would help me. But I must first think it over carefully. Are there really any people left who have the courage to act decently? Father Erwin and Father Lukas are exceptions. They are priests who are willing to take risks. But most lay people are content to be left in peace in the knowledge that they are safe. This is especially true when they do not entirely agree with the things that are happening. I decided to wait a while longer and see what happens.

A period of difficulties and disquiet is behind me. When we left Berlin on June 15, we made it as far as Leipzig. There, we came upon a large refugee transport from Hamburg. Unspeakable misery presented itself to us. The vast concourse of the train station was filled with pitiful people who had managed to save nothing but their naked lives. The adults could rouse little pity in me, unlike the poor, innocent children. Many were without chaperons and sat, ragged and dirty, on the floor. A fair number still had a few possessions they huddled over. There were no signs of Western culture here. We, too, sat among them and waited for daybreak. Silvan slept peacefully on a bed we made from two chairs. We, on the other hand, feared an air raid, which would have been a catastrophe with this number of people. The NSV distributed soup and warm drinks but, even though we were freezing, we did not dare to ask for something warm since I could not be noticed.

We had not yet settled on a destination. It occurred to me to travel to Remagen to my eldest sister. She is also married to an Aryan, and I was hoping that hatred against Jews was not as great in the Catholic Rhineland. At five o'clock in the morning a train happened to go in the direction of Cologne, and happy for the opportunity to escape Leipzig so quickly, we continued on our journey. But in Remagen we found that there was no possibility for us to stay. I wanted to go on to Maria Laach but suddenly I had no energy left to go on another excursion into the unknown. So I telegraphed Father Lukas that we were without shelter and to send word to Remagen. The very next day his message reached us directing us to Reutte in Tyrol, from where I would be able to call him. We immediately set out on the long journey, and in Reutte Father Lukas told me over the telephone to go to Tannheim where a letter from him was already awaiting me. Not knowing what to do next, Father Lukas had driven to Innsbruck to see Bishop Paulus (I had told him in Berlin that the bishop knew me), who, in turn, discussed the situation with my confirmation sponsor Monsignor Weisskopf. The latter suggested the parental home of his pastoral assistant, Sister Claveria, as the safest place for us. Gustav is back in Berlin. He could only stay with us for a few days.

The local baroque church has proved to be a fine consolation to me. Magnificent, vast and dominating the valley, its bells sound marvelously. (Tannheim did not have to give up its bells because of their historical value.[73] They hail from the workshop of the famous bell founder Löffler.) I attend Mass there almost every morning. I often take Silvan who loves this beautiful church very much.

SEPTEMBER 1943

There are two factions in this village: Loyal Catholics and National Socialists. With a curious confidence I single out the people I can safely speak with, and I have yet to make a mistake. I heard that the local mayor, a German, was a committed National Socialist who received his education at the infamous Ordensburg Sonthofen.[74] This is a terrible thing for me because my Jewish heritage is noted on my official registration.

I spoke to the proprietor of the Adler pub after all. He wants to help me. He believes that Mayor Peter did not yet know of my non-Aryan ancestry because, had he known, it was unthinkable that he would have left me in peace. He said that my application for ration coupons, which remains at the local office, posed a constant danger to me since it could still end up in his hands. In that case I would be doomed because Peter was an unscrupulous, fanatic Nazi. The paperwork has to disappear, but how?

OCTOBER 1943

My fear of Peter plagues me day and night. No one has anything good to say about him, and he maltreats everyone who attends church. He must have already noticed me as well because few visitors attend services. (His office is directly across from the church.) On Sundays during Mass, he has the radio blaring from his office or he orders an SA parade with much pomp and circumstance to pass by the church. The faithful are outraged but they cannot do anything about it. In the village I met many nice families and a number of old farmers who know that I am a Jew and whom I immediately trusted. But should anything happen, none of them can help me.

A few days ago, I traveled to Ettal to ask Father Lukas for advice. He was quite startled when he saw me because in the wake of Italy's capitulation, roads and train stations have been under heavy surveillance, and I have to travel without a valid passport. Of course, I prefer to leave my Jewish identification card in the drawer at home. On the street near the cloister, people shouted at me, "There is one of those Italian women," which did not frighten me since I believed it was far less dangerous than the truth. Father Lukas, whom I told about the incident, advised me in all seriousness to dye my black hair blonde but I will wait a while before I do this. Other than that, my trip to Ettal was uneventful. Father Lukas organized a place for me for the night with reliable people. He did not see any possibility other than for me to stay in Tannheim and to get my hands on the incriminating documents. I do not think that is possible though. I left Ettal in a fairly depressed mood. Father Lukas told me upon leaving that he was going to church right away to pray for my safe return to Tyrol. On the road to the train station I had to pass several check points since controls had indeed been stepped up. Everywhere, I showed my invalid, long expired postal identity card.[75] Because it was issued in 1932, it contained no reference to my Jewish ancestry. Strangely, everyone was satisfied with it.

I returned to Tannheim dejected and at a loss as to what to do next. The exchange with Father Lukas in Ettal had not calmed me. I believe Father Lukas has become fearful. The farmers here who are on my side are also pessimistic and advise me to leave. But where do I go? I am completely distraught.

LATE OCTOBER 1943

Adding to all of my misfortunes, I am now in bed with two broken ribs. Since I only injured my left side, I can more or less write with my right hand while lying down.

Ten days ago, I bicycled with Hedwig, a young farmer, to Pfronten where she had made arrangements to procure a cow. We planned on walking our bicycles back and together drive the cow up to Tannheim. But in a narrow section of a steep mountain pass not far from the village, Frau Hedwig, who was a short distance ahead of me, hit her breaks hard. I was forced to overtake her at a high speed and slammed headlong into a wood transporter. I crashed and lost consciousness. They took me to the nearest house and called a doctor, and to my great shock, a military doctor responded a while later but he barely dared to touch me. He must have presumed my injury more severe than it was and wanted to have me transported to the nearest hospital. I had to prevent this from happening at all costs because they would have demanded to see my papers and would not have admitted me, a Jew. In fact, the doctor should not have even attended me. My God, what did I do? One is allowed to dress the wounds of a criminal if he hurts himself, but everyone would have to leave me lying there if they knew that I was a Jew.[76]

Even though I was quite afraid of the military doctor, after mustering all of my powers of persuasion, I convinced him to send me back to my hosts in Tannheim. Because Frau Hedwig also begged him, he promised to organize a ride to our village. It was getting late, and because Frau Hedwig had to head back to Tannheim with her cow, she left me in the care of a woman who took very good care of me even though she was heavy with child. The car that was to take me back to Tannheim did not arrive until evening. Even though the chauffeur drove most carefully on the bumpy road, the journey proved torturous for me as the slightest jolt caused me ghastly pain.

Everyone in Tannheim was very glad to see me when I returned. Because I arrived so late, they feared I had been taken to the hospital after all. Silvan is happy most of all to have his mama back.

Because I cannot move, I am fully dependent on someone else's assistance, which is mortifying but cannot be helped. How lucky that I am able to write, so that at least I can answer Gustav's letters. He must not find out about this accident because I do not want him to worry unnecessarily.

Silvan brings me great joy. He is very concerned about his sick mama. He tells me that he has made new acquaintances, Sefa and Michl,[77] who are most fond of him. They live in the house next door, and once I am well again I must meet them. It appears the boy is in good hands there.

My boy is still pretty helpless and likes to be waited on, especially when he gets dressed. When I told him recently, "You don't need a valet for that," he asked me what a valet was. I wanted to explain it to him and said, "You do know what a valet (*Kammerdiener*) is, don't you?" "Yes," he said, "I know what a St. Bernard (*Bernardiner*) is. He always carries a basket in his mouth and goes shopping for people." There actually is such a St. Bernard dog in the village and despite my miserable condition I had to laugh heartily about this childish association of valet with St. Bernard.

NOVEMBER 1943

I am more or less myself again. I still carry my left arm in a sling but I am able to walk again. I had barely left my bed when Silvan dragged me to see the farmer Michl and his sister Sefa, who keeps house for him. The boy's judgment was true: They are magnificent human beings. I can trust them and shared all of my troubles with them. Sefa knows a retired gendarmerie inspector who works in the mayor's office. She said that he was a good Catholic and perhaps he could help me make the incriminating document disappear. She plans on taking me to his apartment.

A few days ago, Sefa went on a pilgrimage with me to [Bad] Hindelang to visit a miraculous altar dedicated to the Virgin Mary. For me, it was the first pilgrimage of my life. The road was quite icy and this time I almost broke my arm since right at the outset, I fell a couple of times. Sefa commented that I should finally adopt a firm "farmer's" walk rather than saunter carelessly and absentmindedly down the road. In the next village we came upon an elderly retired priest whom we told about our plan. It seems he did not have much confidence in the city dweller and gave me a walking stick so that I could walk more securely on the ice. Old Sefa needed no such thing. She was steady on her feet, which were accustomed to hiking mountains. We proceeded to pray several rosaries along the way, and although I would have much rather gazed dreamily at the landscape, I diligently joined in the recitation. I had never prayed a rosary before, and I soon discovered that concentration and self-control have value in their own right. Even though my prayers were not as profound as those of pious Sefa, I trust that God noticed my good intentions.

It is quite cold here already, and it is snowing. Delighted by so much snow, Silvan is romping around outside. I am not used to winter here. I only ever knew the high mountains during pleasant, warm weather. I spend my days sitting behind the oven with my teeth chattering. I insist that the heating is quite inadequate even though the oven is almost aglow. Frau Binosa is worried that if I am already feeling cold, I could hardly expect to endure the cold alpine winter. She took one look at my "urban" silk hose and promised to get hold of some sheep's wool so that I could knit myself warm stockings. I did get wool, and since I did not know the first thing about knitting, Sefa taught me. Now the second stocking is almost done but I must admit that dear Sefa helped me a great deal, otherwise I would still be at it a year from now.

Sefa accompanied me to the gendarmerie inspector Carpentari, and I presented my request to him. He promised that he would try to get his hands on the folder with the applications for food ration coupons and destroy mine. But when I saw Herr Carpentari again today, he told me that it was quite impossible for him to get hold of the folder because it was in the mayor's office and he had no excuse to ask for it. He saw as the only solution for me to give notice of my departure and leave town, at least for a while. In that case, I would get the incriminating document back. I should destroy it immediately and file a missing document report in my new place of residence. I should then complete a new registration that omitted the byname "Sara," which was mandatory for all Jewish women. As such it is a good solution but where am I to go?

LATE NOVEMBER 1943

My worries are almost killing me, but I cannot continue to hide behind the stove. Therefore, I thought that as a proven athlete (I rode, swam, rowed, and did gymnastics before my troubles began), I should learn to ski. I believed it would help me conquer the difficulties life is hurling at me in abundance. A local carpenter made skis for Silvan and me and we are merrily going up and down the beginner's slope all day long. I have long gotten past feeling cold. The exercise in the cold, pure air refreshes and toughens me. Even in a snowstorm like we had yesterday when none of the farmers ventured out of doors, Silvan and I romped around outside. (It is nice that in spite of my many cares, I have not forgotten how to be young with my boy. I often call him "my little brother" in jest.) Frau Binosa is surprised how well I have adjusted to the mountain climate. If only I did not have to fear the mayor! Whenever I see him, I am terribly frightened. I respond to his "Heil Hitler" with a "Grüss Gott,"[78] which is suspicious in and of itself because almost all of the other evacuees (thank God there are not many in the village) use the "German greeting."

EARLY DECEMBER 1943

God has once again sent help just in time. Yesterday, I unexpectedly received an invitation from Frau Dr. H., a person completely unknown to me, to spend Christmas with her in Salzburg. She told me she learned about me from Father Professor Redlich.[79] I met this Benedictine priest at the same time I made the acquaintance of Father Lukas. He knew about my situation but I had quite forgotten about him. Yet it was through him that help arrived. In mid-December, Silvan and I will travel to Salzburg. I let Gustav know today. He always writes such bleak letters and is so sad about the separation from his boy and me.

The farewell from Tannheim was unspeakably hard for me. A few girls from the village serenaded us before we left. They sang beautiful, old folk songs that I love.

JANUARY 1944

How lucky we are to be allowed to return to Tannheim! We felt quite uprooted in Salzburg. As we left Reutte by bus and Silvan spotted the church steeples of Tannheim from afar he said with a deep sigh: "Now we are finally back home."

We fared very badly in Salzburg. Frau Dr. H., who had invited us, greeted us at the train station with the news that, unfortunately, she was unable to accommodate us after all because there was a chance that both her sons were coming home on furlough from the front. But I am inclined to believe that she regretted her benevolence because we took an instant dislike to each other. We found lodging in a pretty miserable inn. We had no heat in our room during those cold days and mostly roamed around in the streets. This is how we spent Christmas Eve. In my misery, I went to the Benedictine nuns at Nonnberg Abbey and talked with Father Mager.[80] Full of kindness and understanding for our homelessness, he told me that I could not experience Christmas night in a more genuine or profound way than in this moment, since I, too, was on the run from people who shunned me, just like the Virgin Mary. I confessed, and then he gave both of us a small artificial Christmas tree that made Silvan very happy, not in the least because it had little candles on it.

A theology student joined us and together we discussed my dire predicament. We could not stay at the inn. But by far the worst thing was that I had no ration coupons for meals at the tavern since I had "lost" my registration, and I had used up the few travel coupons that I brought with me from Tannheim. Because I could not risk applying to a government office and thereby draw attention to myself (Salzburg is very dangerous for Jews), we decided that the only solution was to return to Tannheim immediately. But right away a new problem presented itself: All private travel had been suspended over Christmas, and it was possible to obtain a travel permit from the police only in the case of an emergency. I lived in great fear of the police since I could not even produce a valid passport. The student would have liked to invite us to his parents' over Christmas but feared there was not enough room because many of his siblings were still at home. I resolutely declined, since I did not want to disturb the family's peace over the holidays. He then offered to go to the police with me and assist me there as much as possible. We set out right away. Father Mager invited us for afternoon tea, at which time we were to give him a report. In the meantime, he would pray that all went well. And indeed, everything did go well. They did not ask very many questions and gave me a travel permit. The afternoon hour with Father Mager was the most peaceful that Silvan and I spent in Salzburg.

In the evening, as we sat in a gloomy mood on our suitcases in front of the train station, Silvan said sadly: "The Christ Child cannot find us today because He does not know where we are."[81] Shortly before the train arrived, the student stopped by to bid us farewell. He had snuck away from the family Christmas festivities to say goodbye to us. He brought cookies and chocolate for Silvan. The boy's face lit up: "Now the Christ Child has found us after all." Unfortunately, I cannot remember the helpful young man's name. We suffered much hunger in Salzburg and experienced much bitterness, but in spite of these hardships, Father Mager and this good man revealed to us the peace and love of Christmas night.

Christmas day, however, proved ever more miserable for us. My thoughts about Tannheim were shrouded in gloom because I feared that the farmers would now be too afraid to welcome us back. For this reason,

I interrupted our journey in Bruckberg, where Father Lukas of Ettal is now the parochial vicar. I wanted to seek his advice but what I already suspected turned out to be true: Father Lukas has become so fearful that he no longer wants anything to do with us. I can hardly comprehend how this helpful priest has turned into someone so cold and hard. We never talked. He only agreed to arrange overnight accommodations for us with a farmer, who showed us to a dark, unheated room. He did not even give us a candle, so that we did not know what the room we stayed in looked like. (I still do not know since we left the room before daybreak.) Telling us that the room had stood empty for several years and would be quite cold, he left us on our own, and we both shivered from the cold the entire night. Never in my life have I felt this cold.

We arrived back in Tannheim in the evening of St. Stephen's Day. Frau Binosa had to take in other guests and no longer had room for us. We reluctantly asked Michl and Sefa if they had room for us, and he and the good Sefa immediately took us in with much love and gave us the best room in the house. We have become members of the family. We live, pray, and eat together with them. There exists a beautiful peace between us. We delight in the knowledge of how well people from the country and the city can get along when there is goodwill.

Sefa was quite shocked that we had to spend most of the Christmas holidays on a train, so she decorated a small tree for us. Thus the Christ Child came to us once more with much love. How wonderful it is that my little boy met these two kind human beings during my illness. I still remember how he dragged me over here one day almost against my will. Otherwise, we would not have known where to turn. Silvan is especially happy that he can be near his Michl. He already talks like Michl, he has the same gait as Michl, he prays like Michl, and, yes, at table he eats like Michl. He now slurps loudly as he spoons his soup, and when I reprimanded him about his ill-mannered way of eating, he retorted: "Michl also eats his soup this way and you said that whatever Michl does is always good." So now he may continue to merrily slurp his soup.

Gustav writes despondent letters. He does not have anyone to talk to. Since I left Berlin he has also given up playing the piano, his only diversion. He says he takes no pleasure in it when he cannot play for me. I wrote to him asking him to take his vacation soon and join us here.

FEBRUARY 1944

I have been taking harmonium lessons from a Catholic sister in order to divert myself a bit and once again to have the opportunity to play music. Playing legato on the harmonium suits me better than playing the piano. Most of all, I can only bear serious music now.

Again there are difficulties. When Sefa registered me, the mayor told her that I had no right to stay in Tannheim since the village was only responsible for evacuees from Innsbruck and Essen. The mayor said that I should return to Berlin from where the NSV would send me somewhere else, but there was no room for me here. Since he does not know that I am a Jew (otherwise he would have behaved very differently toward me), I believe he wants to get rid of a churchgoer. Others who also do not "belong" here but who are good Nazis are allowed to stay.

Now the mayor quartered a family of five, all good National Socialists, with Michl so that there is no longer any room for us. The mayor insists that we leave. What will happen now?

I am expecting Gustav. Michl will keep us here until he arrives. Silvan sleeps in Sefa's room, and I sleep on a bench by the fireplace in the living room. It is somewhat hard and narrow but at least it is under Michl's roof; it means safety.

LATE FEBRUARY 1944

My husband has arrived from Berlin, and Michl shares his room with him. Gustav is thin and looks so haggard. I hardly recognized him. Has it only been half a year since I last saw him? How this evil age can ravage a human being. He is very quiet and reserved, except with Michl. He likes to talk with him. He senses that he is a good person.

Gustav became bedridden just one day after his arrival because he could no longer tolerate hearty food. He never took the time in Berlin to eat a proper meal because he had to prepare it himself and do all the shopping. He thus lived mostly on the inadequate war rations available in the factory's mess. He often stayed at work for days at a time. He spent his days in the laboratory and at night he went on patrol as the air-raid warden. Poor Gustl! Moreover, he had no one to exchange his thoughts with, no relaxation, no rest!

The doctor diagnosed Gustav with a serious stomach ailment, and he had to extend his vacation. Duty called and he was determined to return to Berlin at all costs but it was impossible for him to undertake the long and arduous journey. He remains in bed. What shall become of us? We cannot remain in Tannheim any longer. We have to leave.

EARLY MARCH 1944

Gustav forced himself to get up. Reduced to a skeleton, he walks bent over. Michl and Sefa's concern for him is touching. They constantly feed him good milk, butter, and cheese. And when we visited good old Frau Binosa, who is herself down with a fever, she gave him a few eggs that someone else had given her to hasten her convalescence. When Gustav refused to accept them, she became quite angry and said that he was a young man who had to take care to recover his health. By contrast, she had already fulfilled her purpose in life. Thus, with the help of these good people, Gustav is gradually recovering his strength.

Michl and Sefa thought long and hard as to how they could help us, and Sefa decided to walk to Jungholz to see her brother (a journey of over four hours) to ask him to take us in. The village is located in the county of Sonthofen. The family is willing to host us.

LATE MARCH 1944

Even though Gustav is still very weak, we had to load our belongings onto a sled and move to Jungholz. I cannot quite comprehend how we ended up in such a dreary place. The house is completely neglected and full of dirt from top to bottom. I cleaned our room as best I could but all day long we are plagued by fleas. Below us lives the farmer with his wife and their seven squalid children. We share the first floor with an evacuated woman from Bremen and her four children so that Silvan completes the dozen. For our meals we have to go to the nearby tavern. I usually do not like to eat in a pub. (It also increases the danger for us since we are being seen too often.) But in this case, I prefer it because I could not force down one bite in the home of these dirty people.

In fact, the entire village makes an unkempt and wretched impression, and I cannot shake the feeling of forlornness. I am sure nothing good lies in store for me here, and I want so much to run away, but where would I go? The village is situated on a high plateau, giving one the impression that it is at the mercy of any wind and weather. I feel equally exposed here among the people. Tannheim is situated in a lovely valley surrounded by jagged, impressive mountain ridges that stand like guardians over the village. The landscape by itself roused a sense of safety inside me. Here, the instant I laid eyes on the village, I was struck by a feeling of dread that I have yet to shake.

To secure Silvan's stay and mine at least to some degree, Gustav decided to take me to the county commissioner in Sonthofen.[82] He was encouraged by the local priest who believed this course of action held out some promise. We candidly shared our difficult situation with the commissioner. He is a kind person, ready to help, and has no intentions of expelling me. Nonetheless, he cautioned us that he was powerless if the party learned about me. Since we were unable to make our way back to Jungholz that evening, we decided to spend the night in Sonthofen. But all of a sudden, I started fretting over Silvan, whom I had left in the care of the farmer's wife in Jungholz with the many unruly children. I immediately rang the post office in Jungholz and asked to have the woman brought to the phone. She assured me that Silvan was doing well, but upon our return the next day, he was in bed with a high fever. About one hour prior to my call, he had badly scalded his face, shoulders, and arms with hot coffee. The children were playing in the kitchen and when the woman attempted to put the coffee pot on the table, Silvan ran toward her and spilled the coffee all over him. She hid the truth from me because she did not want to worry me over the phone. A medic from the village administered first aid. Since the burns were quite severe, I called a doctor almost 10 kilometers away. When he did not have time to come up to Jungholz, I bundled the boy in blankets— his fever had reached almost 40 degrees [Celcius]—and drove on a horse sled down the mountain. Two hours later, we reached the doctor. (The path was very steep and the going very slow due to snow drifts.) Since Silvan is a healthy boy, he came through the ordeal just fine. Thank God! Luckily, there seem to be no permanent scars on his face, only on his neck and arm.

EARLY APRIL 1944

Gustav has returned to Berlin. He was even more downcast about our wretched situation than I. His pessimism weighed me down, and I can almost cope better on my own. Our situation is indeed disheartening. It is not just that everything around us is ugly, that we have an awful bedstead, no table at which to occupy ourselves, no stove to heat, so that we are cold, or that we suffer hunger. Rather, what is so hard to bear is that the people we are surrounded by are so cold and unkind. Now the four children next door to us have come down with scabies. Concerned for Silvan, I immediately procured a disinfectant. We often wash our hands with it and asked that the others use this solution as well. Because they will not and since life is otherwise quite unbearable there, I decided to go hiking with Silvan. Though we still have snow, spring will come soon. We will surely find lodging for short periods at a time, and we can hardly fare worse anywhere else than here. Gustav has provided me with enough money to carry on like this for a while. We are registered in Jungholz, and are receiving our badly needed food ration coupons. Other than that it is a good thing that we make ourselves scarce in the village, which is full of out-of-towners.

LATE APRIL 1944

We are once again resting at Michl's for a few days. We have been on the road for almost fourteen days. The roads were mostly bad. At times we waded through nearly meter-high snow. Every step I sank in over my knees, and whenever we reached our destination we were exhausted. Although the hard snow usually held fast until midday, we still broke through it repeatedly. Silvan very bravely held his own and whenever he climbed out of my footsteps he told me: "You must not worry about me. I am very good at this." We spent a few nights in villages that were known to us but then we moved on in order to avoid trouble, as we are no longer even permitted to stay in the County of Reutte. First, we were in the Pfeiffermühle near Jungholz, which is still in Sonthofen County. A room happened to be available for three days. After that we walked to Unterjoch to stay with a fairly nice farmer. He told us that we could stay with him for four days. (It goes without saying that I had to pay him very well.) His boy was coming home on Saturday and needed the room. Thus we moved on to Schattwald where our destination was the "Post," whose proprietor, Josef Fink, I knew through Sefa.[83] The Tyrolean pub owner, who was known to everyone far and wide, was very nice to us. He was sorry to have no room for us but said we could stay in his annex for two days. Then we went to Zöblen where I slept for another two days on a bench near the fireplace in a farmhouse. Silvan stayed on the sofa. On our first day there we hiked up the hill to a chapel near Zöblen dedicated to the Virgin Mary,[84] and on the way there we happened upon a very nicely situated mountain farmstead. Two friendly old women farmed it together with an older male employee. They were sawing wood and because I enjoyed lending a hand at these lofty heights, I sawed alongside them with enthusiasm. The old women invited us later for a bite to eat but I was too embarrassed to accept such a reward for my labors and to sidestep the issue told them that Silvan and I still wanted to go up to the little chapel. However, upon our return, one of the women stood outside of the house waiting for us. She pressed us to come inside and invited us to eat with them. A good farmer's loaf, golden butter, and honey stood next to fresh milk on the nicely set table. These friendly old women instantly took a liking to Silvan, and I found it easy to converse with them. I was honest and told them why we were on the road. They were quite touched and kindly offered us their hospitality. Even though they had little room, they insisted that we remain as their guests for a few days. We thus stayed on the mountain for another four days. I joyfully labored alongside them. I once again sawed wood, spread manure on the sunny mountain slope where the snow cover had started to recede, and fed the cows.

Tired from our travels, we are glad to rest again in Michl's place for a few days. He hopes that no one will make any trouble for us for such a short period of time. But we are apprehensive and only seldom show ourselves in the village.

Happy news awaited us at Michl's. Father Erwin wrote to me from Berlin that he planned on spending his upcoming holiday in Bad Hindelang; he wanted to meet with us.

The police came by today to let us know that Silvan and I had to leave Tannheim immediately. If I were not gone by tomorrow noon, the police would deport me to Berlin. Thus, we must once more fasten our bundles. We live worse than gypsies; at least they have a horse and wagon and people do not despise them like they do us.[85]

Before leaving, we visited the grave of Frau Binosa to bring her some flowers. She recently passed away. We owe her so much; she was always good to us.

EARLY MAY 1944

We are staying for a few days at an inn near the train station in Nessel-wang. Everything is quite uncomfortable here but the people seem decent. As we turned eastward from Tannheim, we came over the narrow pass to Pfronten, where we tried in vain to find lodging for a few days. Tired from the taxing hike (I always have to drag along a heavy backpack because Silvan and I need several weeks' worth of clothing), I went from house to house, but everywhere we were met with nothing but suspicious questions and contemptuous faces. Exhausted and filled with fear of the approaching night, we decided to take the train one station farther to Nesselwang. How glad we were when we were kindly received there.

I phoned the parish office in Hindelang today. Father Erwin has already arrived, and I was able to speak with him on the telephone. He is spending his vacation in Imberg, near Sonthofen. He is expecting us and we will go there in the next few days.

LATE JUNE 1944

We are back in Jungholz. Has it really only been two months since we left Jungholz? So much has happened since, and I have the feeling years have passed.

We were overjoyed when we arrived in Imberg at the beginning of May. Silvan was especially happy to see Uncle Erwin. We were lucky and found short-term lodging with a local farmer. We had a lovely time. Father Erwin is just as I remembered him. He is devoted to us and we spent most of our time in his company. Upset about my unsettled life, he tried to cheer me up. He played with Silvan as in old times, sang jolly songs, and was in the mood for all kinds of pranks. This is how we spent a few peaceful days. Every morning he said Mass in a small chapel, and I received Holy Communion from him.

Toward the end of his vacation he went on a pilgrimage with me to Bad Hindelang. For days I had been dwelling on the hopelessness of my situation. What will happen to us? I was gripped by a great anguish because soon (we could stay in our room for only a few more days) we once again had to face the unknown. Just thinking about Jungholz caused me terrible agony. I thought that by himself Silvan could probably stay with the farmer in Imberg. He would be in good hands there. I managed to deceive a doctor and obtained digitalis.[86] I did not want to be hunted any longer. Father Erwin took me on the pilgrimage because he had suspected for some time that something was wrong. When he learned of the digitalis he was horrified and reprimanded me. He demanded that I hand the poison over to him and urged me to let go of these terrible thoughts. That evening I gave the bottle to him, and the next day he accompanied me to church in Sonthofen where I went to confession. Because he had a prior engagement, Father Erwin stayed in Sonthofen and I climbed back up the hill to Imberg. On the way, I was once again gripped by such fear of the future that I had a change of heart. Feigning heart troubles, I asked Father Erwin's hostess Frau Dinser for the bottle of digitalis.[87] As I suspected, it was in Father Erwin's room, and I claimed that he had obtained it for me. Not suspecting anything, she gave me the medication. Tired and defeated, not even the thought of Silvan, who was already asleep, could stop me from drinking the entire bottle.

Because I told Frau Dinser that I was unwell and my lodging was quite far away, she urged me to lie down on the sofa in her living room. Frau Dinser later sat down beside me, and since she is such a kind, motherly woman, she was very concerned about me.

She sensed my agitation and asked what was wrong with me. Overcome by a sudden and terrible fear, I told her everything. She was shocked and immediately got in touch with Father Erwin who, in an unbelievably short amount of time, made his way up the hill. When he arrived the poison was already taking effect. My legs and arms became heavy and I could not shake my fear. Frau Dinser later told me how greatly I had disappointed Father Erwin and how appalled he was by my wrongdoing, and I sincerely regretted that I had offended this good and benevolent man. He tried to get me to make a remorseful confession but I felt no remorse. My fear of the future was too great. Later my tongue ceased to function and I could barely talk. I can still recall everything clearly because I was completely aware of my surroundings. I remember that I said over and over how I feared the emptiness into which I was about to plunge. Father Erwin knelt down and prayed with me but the terror I felt did not diminish. By morning, he felt that the crisis had passed, and I fell into a restless sleep. The dose had not been strong enough.

Because he had to return to Berlin, Father Erwin asked Frau Dinser to look after me. I owe it to her selfless care that after three weeks I could once again walk, and even though I was still quite weak I did not want to burden these good people any longer and decided to return via Bad Hindelang to Jungholz. In Bad Hindelang I hoped to catch the bus that would take us over the Oberjochpass. But when we arrived in the village, we learned that the bus had stopped running for a few days because it needed repairs. I was exhausted from the strenuous walk, and not knowing what to do next, I took Silvan to the rectory and explained my situation to the priest there.[88] Since the rectory was quite large, he offered Silvan and me a room. He tried to assure me that the bus would surely start running again soon, and until then, my boy and I could live with him since it was impossible for me to hike the steep Oberjochpass in my condition. But when the bus was still not running two days later, he started to fear that the police could learn about us (I had told him that I was a Jew), and without further ado, he cast us out into the pouring rain. He remarked that he had been quite good to us for two days (we shared his meals and he refused to accept payment) but now we had to move on. He was sorry that the weather was so bad and that I felt so miserable. As we stood in front of the rectory, I said to Silvan that we had been beggars here, and I went inside the church to deposit the money that the priest had refused to accept from me into the poor box.

In arduous, exhausting stages, I dragged myself back to Jungholz. I did it for the sake of my boy whose trust I must not betray. As always, he was very concerned about me. Here, in this miserable shack, on the uncomfortable bed, and amid the noise that twelve children make, it is impossible to rest and convalesce. Hopefully, the damage I did to my heart is not permanent. We will move on as soon as I have recovered some of my strength.

EARLY JULY 1944

I had to enroll Silvan in school, which starts in the fall. Now the village teacher, who goes to Mass every day, tells me that he can hardly be expected to teach a half-Jewish boy. He wants to report the case to his superiors.[89] What will happen now? If he accepts the boy, then we are condemned to stay in this wretched place. Furthermore, I will be forced to perform compulsory labor. For a Jew, this means internment in a camp. At the very least, local authorities will learn of my non-Aryan heritage. (The people I live with know that I am a Jew.) If he can refuse to take the boy, then others here will not leave us in peace either.

At this very inopportune time, Gustav announced that he was coming for a visit. He wants to take his furlough at the end of the month to check on us. Apparently, Father Erwin told him about what happened and he worries about me. This is wholly unnecessary since I have pulled myself together and know that I must persevere for as long as I can be of help to Silvan and not too much of a burden to Gustav.

Tomorrow, we will move on in the hope of finding reasonably comfortable lodging for the fourteen days that Gustav will spend with us.

BEGINNING OF AUGUST 1944

We went to meet Gustav in Bad Hindelang, and spent eight peaceful days in Hinterstein, approximately two hours from Bad Hindelang. Then we had to return to Jungholz, and Gustav wanted to spend what was left of his holiday here because all this wandering about tires him out.

Today I received notification from the county commissioner in Sonthofen that I had to leave Jungholz and the region of Sonthofen within twenty-four hours, lest I be "expelled by the police in case of noncompliance." The teacher also handed me a form stating that on account of "special circumstances," Silvan's enrollment in school had been deferred. The good man surely had no idea that this document could be my salvation. Now I can inform the authorities that I have a child who is not yet of school age and hence I will be exempt from compulsory labor. I will homeschool my child myself.

Starting tomorrow we must once again wander into the unknown. The worst thing about the situation is that we have to deregister with the

neans we will not get any more ration coupons. And
to register again?

LATE AUGUST 1944

again in Nesselwang. I have avoided registering so far
ause I heard that the party is quite active here. But I will not be able
to keep this up for long. Gustav is back in Berlin. He was here for a few
more days, and we accompanied him as far as Kempten from where he
continued on home. Gustav was very discouraged and did not believe
that we could remain in this area for much longer. He thinks we have to
return to Berlin. That would mean the end for Silvan and me.

Because our ration coupons are almost gone we have to register somewhere but here it is impossible. In my despair, today I went to see the local
priest, Father Huber, and asked for advice.[90] He told me to go to Pfronten
where the mayor was Catholic and not a member of the party. I should
go and talk to him. So tomorrow we will go to Pfronten. Even though
I do not have very good memories of the place I have no other choice.

LATE SEPTEMBER 1944

So far most of our stay here in Pfronten has been very hard. After knock-
ing in vain on many doors in Pfronten-Kreuzegg we found temporary
lodging with inconsiderate and greedy people. As we encountered cold
and hostile faces at every door, I said to Silvan that people were very evil.
He replied indignantly: "No, mama, you must not say that all people are
evil because Michl and Sefa are good people." When I did not reply in
my misery: "Mama, you have to agree, don't you?" Yes, poor, little Silvan.
Yet most people are evil. Once again, we learned how hard people can
be. For lunch I had to make a two-hour round-trip with my boy to the
closest pub. Even in exchange for good pay and ration coupons, which I
was able to give her because she had registered me properly, the farmer's
wife refused to give us anything to eat. I have to make this long trek even
in the pouring rain. Only reluctantly did she permit me to make some
tea for us on her stove in the evening. Then catastrophe struck: I became
ill and had to remain in bed. Since I had no desire to eat, I was not lacking
anything, but they fed my small boy only most unwillingly and he often

suffered hunger there. Once he came to my bed after returning from herding cows (every morning he drove out the cows with the cowherds) and told me that on the way he was so hungry that he lay down beneath a cow and milked her into his mouth. Quite a lot had come "out." How easily the cow could have injured him. I was shocked. This could not continue. I was getting weaker in bed, and as soon as the farmer's wife told us that she no longer felt like hosting us because she had heard we were Jews, I gathered all my strength and went to Pfronten to see the mayor,[91] whom the priest of Nesselwang had recommended to us. It took me over two hours to make my way there. The mayor was a good and kind old gentleman, whom I immediately trusted. I told him that I was a Jew and about what happened to me in Kreuzegg. He replied that I had encountered the wrong people, and when he saw how much strength it cost me just to keep myself upright, he exclaimed that I was sick. He made it his priority to get my boy and me admitted to the local hospital,[92] which was now a field hospital. He assured me that the Catholic sisters there would find a way to care for us. He phoned the mother superior,[93] and after telling her the most basic facts, he indicated that he wanted to send us to her right away. Turning toward me he said—with tears running down his cheeks—that he wanted to continue to care for us poor, harassed people as best as he could. But first we should go to the sisters.

The mother superior of the Sisters of Mercy was a very good and understanding woman. She said that she could not admit me to the field hospital because it was entirely filled with soldiers, but there was an adjacent orphanage, and perhaps she could find a place for us there. She had the children's nurse, Ingeborg,[94] called over, who immediately agreed to give up her own room and move into the children's dormitory for a while. She also promised to move a children's bed for Silvan into the room. We spent two quiet weeks there while I quickly recovered my strength. The children's nurse became my dear friend. Because she cared for us so lovingly, I completely regained my health and was able to move in with a farmer and his family in Pfronten, to whom the good sister recommended us. Silvan's cheeks have also become chubby again.

I almost had another accident in the narrow pass. Most of my luggage was still in Tannheim (part of it was in Jungholz and part in Nesselwang), and because we were in urgent need of some things, I rode in a light hunting carriage from Pfronten to Jungholz to fetch what I needed. A young woman who owned the horse accompanied me and drove the carriage. In the narrow pass, the young and very nervous horse became skittish and nearly turned the wagon over very close to the spot where I had crashed my bicycle a year earlier. Once the owner of the horse lost control of it, she became scared and refused to go any farther. But why had I learned to ride and handle horses if not for situations such as these? Without further ado, I took hold of the reins and managed to calm the animal. It willingly yielded to my guidance and we arrived safely in Tannheim. Since the young woman had lost her nerve, I drove the wagon almost the entire 20 kilometers home. I was so worn out from the exertion that I could barely keep my eyes open that evening.

We live with fairly friendly people and eat in the local pub. I hope things stay this peaceful. At midday Silvan plays with the children at the orphanage. I have to go with him since he does not enjoy himself otherwise, and when I do not play with them, I mend the poor children's socks. All the little rascals like Aunt Erna and often mind her better than the sisters. The children are often a thorn in the sisters' side. Most of them hail from derelict homes or have behavioral problems. It is understandable that the sisters believe Silvan is practically an angel (but he really is not one), and they spoil him accordingly. He visibly basks in the sisters' praise, and the good children's nurse always saves a bit of lunch so that Silvan keeps his chubby cheeks despite the sparse pub provisions. The children are splendidly cared for, and they all look very well fed. Many children are picky and refuse to eat certain things, unlike Silvan who gladly eats what is put in front of him.

LATE OCTOBER 1944

Now any peace we had is once again at an end. I have been quite anxious lately and have phoned Berlin often. Gustav thus was able to inform me that at the end of October he would be interned in a forced labor camp.[95] He did not know where. I asked him if I should come to Berlin for a few days before his internment but he declined out of concern for me. I nonetheless felt duty bound at least to stand by him during his last days in

Berlin. Once the orphanage agreed to take care of Silvan during my absence, I decided to travel to Berlin without any papers.

Fully cognizant of the dangers that awaited me on my journey (bombing raids, arrest because I had no papers, or betrayal by my dear neighbors), I conferred with the orphanage's spiritual adviser, who promised me to keep special watch over Silvan should anything happen to me.

I first traveled to Augsburg where I hoped to catch an express train to Berlin. The concourse was filled with people, and when a train arrived that went in the direction of Berlin, the crowd stormed the doors. It was impossible to get on. Two hours later, already past midnight, another train going toward Berlin arrived, and I was determined not to let it pass by under any circumstances. Again everyone rushed the doors. I stood quite restlessly on the platform when an officer standing in the train car let down the window and asked if I wanted to come along. When I answered in the affirmative, he said that he could pull me in through the window if I was limber enough. The window was quite high up, but I barely gave it a thought because I was happy for the opportunity to get on board. Telling him that I was a seasoned gymnast, he gave me his hand and I swung myself through the window. A lady standing next to me attempted to follow suit but she could not pull herself up and had to abandon her quest to get on. Now that I was inside I had just enough room to put both my feet on the ground. I was certainly safe from passport controls here since conducting any checks would have been quite impossible in this crowded situation. Besides, the inside of the train, just like the outside, was pitch black on account of the looming danger of air raids. After standing in one spot all night, I arrived in Berlin around 10:00 a.m. I was dead tired but nonetheless I went straight to Gustav at his workplace.

Since I could not go inside his laboratory for fear of informers, I had him called outside. His immense joy in seeing me was instantly overshadowed by concern for my safety, and he told me that I could under no circumstances risk going home. It was too dangerous on account of our "dear" neighbors. So I decided to go and see Frau Herberg. Since Gustav had to go back to work, I planned on waiting for him there. She would certainly know what to do. Frau Herberg was genuinely glad to see me again and there was no question that I would be her guest. When Gustav arrived in the evening, she invited him to stay as well, and we spent six days together in this hospitable home before Gustav had to report to a camp near Nikolassee. I went with him to the barbed wire fence where we had to separate. Poor Gustav! You have to endure this on my account and I cannot help you. Even if I sacrificed my own life, I could not give you back your freedom. Gustav urged me to bear everything with courage for the sake of our child. He must survive. And so, two hours later, I once again traveled south to my boy.

Father Erwin accompanied me to the train station to give me courage. On our last evening, he had sat with us until late into the night consoling us both.

These few days in Berlin depressed me terribly. Many destroyed homes! Entire blocks have been razed. As I traveled on the tram through Berlin to get to the Anhalter train station, I often had to close my eyes because I simply could not bear all this destruction. Once, as darkness set in, I briefly went to our apartment—no one saw me—where I packed the most essential items for Gustav. How grim our home looks! In all of the rooms, the furniture is covered with thick dust. The walls sported large cracks from the tremors caused by the many bombs that had fallen nearby. Debris and mortar litter the carpets. The blackout curtains are drawn over most windows so that no daylight can filter in. In the bathroom and kitchen, the windowpanes were shattered. It is of course impossible to get glass anywhere. To keep the cold at bay, Gustav has covered some of the openings with boards. He had to live in this squalid place for quite some time. This must have been especially hard for him since he was used to a well-cared-for home. He never had time to make any repairs to the house because he often spent his days and nights at the plant, and whenever he did not have to spend his free time in the air-raid shelter, he tried to catch some badly needed sleep. It has been impossible for him to find help because who would still set foot in our home? Thus our home steadily falls into ruin. None of the doors close anymore. All the furniture is damaged; the rear panel of the piano has been blown off. The tremors have caused many of the glasses, crystal objects, and fine porcelain in the vitrine to break. All the mirrors are shattered. But does any of this matter anymore now that we have been so mercilessly torn apart?

The first thing that awaited me here on my return was a message that we had to leave Pfronten. The mayor sent word to me that the party knew about me and wanted to make my life difficult.

Even though I did not arrive until evening, I immediately went to see my son in the orphanage. How happy he was to see me. In the eight days that I was away, Silvan has become pale and thin. The sister told me that he hardly ate anything and refused to play. The child is usually so lively, but he was so plagued by homesickness that he developed a fever and had to be put to bed. So I must abandon my plan to leave Silvan in the care of the sisters while I set out alone into the unknown.

Dear God, what will become of us? I have no idea where to go. Shall I try to go to Michl for a few days? Perhaps he has some advice. Even though I fear the police there, I see no other possibility.

NOVEMBER 1944

Even though we have been in Tannheim less than a week, and I have barely dared to set foot outside the door, the police came by during lunch today to chase us out with all kinds of threats. What should I do? Michl was at a loss as well. At four in the afternoon a bus leaves for Reutte, and we are taking it. God must show us a way forward.

CHRISTMAS 1944

The manner in which we have been driven from place to place! Now I am sick in bed in the Sonne tavern in Häselgehr. What a Christmas! Our room is freezing, the damp walls glisten, and I am in bed with a fever of nearly 40 degrees Celsius. Still, we must be grateful to have a roof over our heads. Silvan goes into the homes of strangers to warm himself, and fortunately, he has warm clothing. I am still feeling quite faint even though my fever has started to come down and the pain when I breathe is less severe.

The road to this place has been arduous and long. When I traveled to Reutte in November, I followed Michl's advice and sought out the local priest there.[96] He gave me a letter of recommendation addressed to the priest in Bach im Lechtal[97] and warned me that under no circumstances was I to remain in Reutte because the district commissioner lived here and dealt with Jews harshly.[98] After kind people hosted us for the night, we set out for Lechtal the following afternoon. My heart was heavy with worry, and I intuitively knew that the priest in Bach would not help me. In my fear and restlessness, I started a conversation with an elderly man sitting next to me, in an attempt to sound him out about available accommodations in Lechtal. The man was very friendly, and throwing all caution to the wind, I told him right there in the overcrowded bus that I was a Jew and that I was being chased about in the most dreadful manner. He responded that he was a baker who was known throughout Lechtal. He wanted to try to help me, and I was to let him know if the priest in Bach could not assist me.

We did not reach Bach that evening. Shortly before the bus driver reached Häselgehr, the darkness (because of the danger of air raids he had to drive without headlights) and high snow caused him to lose his bearings and drive the bus over the curb. We almost plunged down the mountain but the bus got stuck, and all the passengers had to get off and make their way through meter-high snow to the next village where we spent the night. I was so glad that I had confided in the man next to me. I could not have found my own way in the darkness. Everyone else was preoccupied, but he took Silvan, who almost disappeared in the high snow, on his shoulders and led us to the nearest tavern where he made sure that we were given a room. He also organized a horse and sleigh to take us to Bach the next day, and he told us that if we could not stay in Bach, we were to come back to the priest in Häselgehr and confide in him. He could not take us in himself because he was already hosting guests in his home.

The priest in Bach had no compassion for us and sent us away. We rode back to Häselgehr on the sleigh. Quite disheartened, I went to the church with Silvan, but lo and behold, what did we find? The walls sported magnificent copper engravings from the Old Testament. To see authentic Jewish figures was a great joy! A priest who is surrounded by such things every day has to be good to us. Full of confidence, I knocked on the rectory's door. The priest was out of town but we spoke with the parochial vicar, Herr Berger,[99] who immediately agreed to help us. He suggested that I leave Silvan at the rectory and seek out the priest in Stanzach,[100] which was situated at the fork of a tributary valley where I could easily be hidden on a lonely, remote farm. But I made the 20-kilometer journey in vain that day, and exhausted I returned to my boy. Father Berger then proposed to take us to Bschlabs the next morning, a tiny village situated high up in a far-flung tributary valley. The priest there was also the owner of the only local tavern, and he could certainly take us in without registering us since hardly anyone went there in the winter. There was also enough food. The farmers would make sure of it. But he cautioned us that we had a hike of five hours through a lot of snow ahead of us. He feared that it would be too much for Silvan, but I assured him that we were used to walking.

He permitted us to spend the night in the rectory. Silvan stayed in the housekeeper's room on a small sofa, and I slept in the absent priest's office on the couch. Even though there was very little room and they were not at all prepared for guests, they overcame these difficulties with their kindness. We left for Bschlabs the next morning immediately after Mass, full of hope of finally finding peace there. The hike was grueling. On one occasion, an avalanche roared down the mountain a few meters behind us. We did not immediately recognize the danger we were in (it was the first time I had seen an avalanche) but the priest did and was terrified. How easily it could have swept us away.

Upon our arrival, we suffered a great disappointment. The pastor, a short man with a high-pitched voice (I immediately disliked him a great deal), was afraid of the party.[101] Despite Father Berger's coaxing and an empty house save the housekeeper, he refused to let us stay. Because he had to celebrate Mass the next morning, Father Berger had to descend the mountain that same afternoon. The pastor would have liked to send us away with him but Father Berger protested vigorously that he should at least have compassion for the child and keep us up there for a few days since we were very tired from the exhausting climb. Father Berger told us to come and see him soon, and he promised to search for a place for us in the meantime. That night there was a terrible storm. It howled and thundered. We could not sleep, and in the morning the priest told us that several avalanches had come down that night and we had to hike back down the mountain straightaway before the entire trail became obstructed. Some parts had already become impassable. Two men with shovels accompanied us and the priest, too, came along for part of the way. He was visibly relieved to be rid of the Jews that had proved such a burden to him.

Now and then, huge masses of snow blocked the way and the two men frequently had to dig a path for us. Time and again an avalanche thundered toward the valley. Whereas at such dangerous passages Father Berger had taken Silvan firmly by the hand and made sure that I, too, kept up, the "courageous" pastor merely called out: "Please hurry up. It is especially dangerous here." He made sure to get himself to safety without any regard for how I struggled to get Silvan past these difficult spots.

I was deadly tired when I arrived with Silvan in Häselgehr. Father Berger was surprised that the priest in Bschlabs had sent us back so quickly and commented on the latter's lack of courage. He invited us to stay at the rectory until the local priest returned from Innsbruck. I had overtaxed myself to such an extent that I had to lie down right away, but Silvan had taken the exertion in stride. That evening I caused my hosts to worry when I experienced severe heart pains. When Father Innerhofer unexpectedly returned home, Father Berger told him about me. He was completely in agreement with the arrangement. Father Innerhofer was also more than willing to help and told me not to be afraid. He would not chase my child and me away, and Father Berger was glad to give up his room to us for a while. The parochial vicar would sleep in his office. During the night, my condition worsened so considerably and the priest was so concerned, he sat by my bed almost the entire night. My body was racked by a serious case of typhoid fever, and for almost three weeks I could not leave the bed. During that time, the priest's sister, the kind Zita, showed such touching concern for Silvan, she completely took over my role as his mother. During my illness, I became very fond of this child of God.

While I was sick, Father Innerhofer attended to me with much selflessness. Whenever darkness began to set in, I was overcome by a dreadful fear, and after asking him to turn on a light, each evening he faithfully turned on several lamps, the large overhead light, a bedside lamp, and the lamp on the desk. I rested the entire night in this radiant brightness. When he noticed that I was troubled by unease and fear, he sat down at the harmonium and beautifully played Beethoven, Bach, Haydn, and, first and foremost, Bruckner. Only once did his recital upset me terribly, when he answered my wish and played the Good Friday Spell and the Grail Motif from Richard Wagner's *Parsifal*. It reminded me so much of the peaceful days I had spent with Gustav, who had also often played pieces from *Parsifal*. Even back then these pieces moved me, but now they overwhelmed me so completely that I suffered a relapse. Since that day, he never played Wagner again.

Because I still suffered from frequent heart pains even after my fever fell, Father Innerhofer skied to Elbigenalp to fetch medicine for me from the local doctor there.

(The doctor himself could not make the journey to see me because he himself was ill, and besides, I, as a Jew, had no right to ask it of him in the first place.) My luggage was also taken care of. Father Berger made a special trip to Tannheim to fetch it for me.

The people in the rectory were all so very kind to us, I felt almost ashamed. Indeed, once I was able to leave my bed, I became truly distressed because I soon noticed that they were quite worried that the police, whose offices were located directly next to the rectory, might find out about me and make difficulties. In fact, once I was feeling slightly better they told me as much without mincing words and suggested that I move to an inn. But it was this I feared most because staying at an inn was far more dangerous for us than moving to a farm, for example. At the inn we were bound to attract much more attention. Besides, I have to list my maiden name on the hotel registration, and, since it is a Jewish name, I always have to misspell it, which troubles me.

Nonetheless, I soon moved to the Sonne Inn, where I came down with the flu and had to take to my bed again.

JANUARY 1945

Again we have to take flight. Once I was able to leave my sickbed, I had no choice but to spend my days in the inn's dining room since our room was so very cold and could not be heated. Unfortunately, the village gendarme, whom I feared terribly, ate his lunch at the Sonne Inn every day.

EARLY FEBRUARY 1945

There is no more peace for us anywhere. We have been here for just fourteen days and already we have to move on. Yes, we have been expelled from the Reutte district once and for all. Dear God, where can we go? Where? If you want us to live, then help us. I am at the end of my wits. Feeling helpless, I turned to the Baker Saurer from Elbigenalp. He took us to the local priest,[102] and persuaded him in the name of God to take us in. He did, but only for two weeks. After that, we had to promise him to seek out the district commissioner in Reutte, tell him about our situation, and ask for permission to remain in the rectory at Elbigenalp. Did this not mean that I would be wandering straight into the den of the lion? What should I do? I promised to go after fourteen days, and yesterday I made the bitter journey. Any success? The district commissioner was a hard man who answered my pleas to take pity on my child with orders to leave his district at once. Staring straight ahead, he eventually showed me the door.

I am on the verge of collapsing. Because my heart is once again giving me a lot of trouble and since I have to leave Elbigenalp this afternoon, I conquered my fear and confided in the local doctor this morning. Against my expectations, he turned out to be quite pleasant. Still, he regretted that he could not do anything for me since my only hope for recovery was immediate admission to a sanatorium where I would need to rest for half a year. But there was no place where he could send a Jew. I had suffered damage to my heart, probably from the large dose of digitalis but also from my unsettled life, and he warned me that I could not endure this chase for another six months.

But I must move on for my child's sake. We leave most of our luggage here and take only what is absolutely necessary in a rucksack. With her quiet demeanor, the priest's cook Rosa has done many good deeds for Silvan and me, and for this she has my particular gratitude. The priest is a very irritable, jittery person. He is fearful and reticent. Silvan feared him but in truth he was good to us. After all, he had his piano put in my room so that I could play and divert myself a bit. When we returned from the tavern at midday, he often inquired whether we had had enough to eat. Frau Rosa, however, cooked a hearty meal for us every evening. When I was laid up for a few days because of a recurring paralysis in my left leg that is terribly painful, it was Frau Rosa who cared for Silvan and me.

The condition of my leg is an entirely new worry. All of a sudden, I have great difficulties walking. After walking for a while, my left leg suddenly becomes stiff and almost impossible to move. Just one more reason to fear the continued wandering from place to place.

FEBRUARY 1945

We have once more found refuge in Tannheim, at least for a few days. I also found letters from Gustav waiting for me there. In one of the letters he wrote to Michl that he had learned that Silvan and I had died in an air raid. He obviously wants to cover our tracks, and I have to find a way to answer him without drawing attention to myself. In the next letter, also addressed to the farmer, he wrote that he was sick. After lingering for weeks in the camp's infirmary with a high fever and severe back pain, he was transferred to the university hospital in Halle.[103] He wrote that he was still in a lot of pain and had a high fever. He longed for fruit and something to drink. The doctors have not yet found the cause of his illness. I already sent two packages to the camp in Merseburg with sausages, bacon, and baked goods.[104] (I had saved my ration coupons.) Now Gustav writes to me that the SS took the sausages and bacon from his package but he did receive the baked goods.

This letter upset me terribly. When I wanted to come to Gustav's aid, dear Sefa was once again our saving grace. She organized apples for Gustav, which was not easy since fruit does not grow in Tannheim. She also fetched the last bottle of wine from the cellar and gave it to me. I had already baked cookies for Gustav at Baker Saurer's bakery in Elbigenalp. I had also saved meat coupons so that I could buy a bit of sausage, and in the end I was able to send him a large package. Hopefully this time they will give him these things. But even in the hospital he is most likely nothing more than a prisoner.

The past few nights I secretly sat by the radio and listened to illegal foreign broadcasts. If everything they are saying is true then this horrible war has to come to an end soon, and with its end will come my liberation.

Today the police made a great commotion at Michl's because of me. How could I dare to show myself in Tannheim even though I had been expelled? We can really no longer remain in Tannheim.

EARLY MARCH 1945

In Elbigenalp, I was given the advice to go to Zams to see Herr Primarius Prenner, who, I was told, was very helpful.[105] Hence, we decided to try our luck there. First we went back to the station tavern in Nesselwang but we stayed for only two days. The police there were conducting checks, which we escaped only by pure chance. We did not feel safe there, but before we left, Silvan and I went once more to see Father Huber, a diocesan official.[106] He had been worried about us and was happy to see us again. He assured us that it would not take much longer and we needed to be brave. He also inquired after the state of my finances. Even though I told him that I had enough money, he insisted that I might need more and gave me 500 marks.[107] Embarrassed, I hesitated before I accepted it. This was the first material aid I had received from a stranger. He said the money had been given to him for a good cause and this way it was well spent.

The trip to Zams proved extraordinarily difficult for us. We planned on taking the train to Ehrwald and from there the bus over the Fernpass to Imst. From Imst it is two stops to Zams. Consulting my map, I decided this was the best way to go. We reached Ehrwald via train but when we tried to transfer to the bus we learned that it only runs on Wednesdays and Saturdays. We were there on a Monday and would have had to wait two days in Ehrwald. Though it was still early in the morning, we immediately looked for lodging. We went from one inn to the next, and there are many in Ehrwald, but everywhere we were told the same thing: the entire village was filled to the last bed with evacuees. We also tried private homes but again without any luck. Eventually, for 60 marks, the proprietor of a small inn offered to take us with her horse and sleigh up the Fernpass. According to her only a few guests stayed in the large hotel up there and we could spend two days there until the bus came by. Glad to have found a solution that allowed us to swap the streets for a roof over our heads, I accepted the offer. I had no idea what new difficulties I was stumbling into. Starving and half frozen, we reached the pass in the afternoon after a nearly four-hour sleigh ride. The large hotel appeared inviting and we looked forward to a heated room and a warm meal. Several gentlemen scrutinized us at length as we entered. It struck me that they thought us modest hikers, with our rucksacks and accompanied by the farmer's wife (who had driven us and whom I had invited to dinner before she had to make the difficult journey back), as somewhat out of place in this elegant hotel. But after all, there is a war on. Appearances no longer matter, so I calmly sat down at a table with Silvan and the farmer's wife. I asked the hostess for something to eat but she replied that there was no food and all they could serve us was a cup of coffee. (The gentlemen, however, did not look like they were suffering from hunger.) In response to my inquiry as to whether my boy and I could take a room until Wednesday until the bus came, she retorted that this was completely out of the question but it was only four hours to Nassereith, and if we left immediately, we would perhaps reach it before dark. Finally, one of the gentlemen joined in the conversation, demanding to know what we were doing up here in the first place. He suspected that something was not quite right with me otherwise I would not be roaming around in these parts. I should take care to move on with my boy or they would have a look at my papers. I was completely intimidated and, without saying a word, I stepped outside with Silvan into the biting winter cold. The ice covering the roads was smooth as glass. Clasping each other's hands, we slowly began to walk away from the inn. Hot tears ran down my cheeks. How hard these people were! We frequently fell on the icy roads, and it was almost a miracle that we arrived safe and sound, after a nearly six-hour hike, late in the evening in Nassereith. We found lodging in the Alten Post Inn. Sensing that we were among decent people, we told them about our experience. They told us that the Fernpass Hotel was occupied by high-ranking SS personnel.

Two days later, we continued our journey to Zams through Imst.

In Zams we found ourselves quite abandoned. Dr. Prenner could not help us and sent us to the local priest,[108] who organized a room for us at the home of a civil servant working for the railways. We stayed eight days and had to eat in the tavern.

Zams was a town on edge. Because of the large factories located in Landeck, there were frequent air-raid alarms. Even though no bombs fell on the village, the population was quite agitated. Silvan and I were unfazed since we were used to much worse from our time in Berlin. On one occasion we went to the public air-raid shelter. It was carved out of the mountain and located deep beneath the hospital that was now a field hospital. There were long corridors and large open spaces that were occupied mainly by the wounded. As we took in everything we started to feel as if we had been buried alive. Since being imprisoned is not at all my thing (they had wardens there), we left the cellar, despite multiple warnings, and climbed up the mountain. But soon after we came outside, a piece of shrapnel from an antiaircraft gun landed on the ground very close to us. Good thing it did not land on our heads! Still, we felt much better up there. The pounding of the antiaircraft guns and the humming of the enemy planes hardly bothered us. From that day on, we went up the mountain every time there was an alarm.

During one of these hikes, Silvan injured himself below his eye with a stick that he, the "mountain climber," insisted on carrying. I went to Dr. Prenner who asked that I consult an eye specialist. He wanted to send me to Innsbruck, but then he remembered that a professor of ophthalmology had recently opened an office in Hatting. (On account of the air raids he had taken refuge there from Innsbruck.) He suggested I go there to avoid getting caught in an air raid. Thus, we went to Hatting. Luckily, Silvan's eye was uninjured. From Hatting, it is two hours to Pettnau and since I had to leave Zams in two days, I decided to pay a visit. Maybe the farmers would still remember me. Even though it had been almost four years since we had been in Pettnau,[109] the village welcomed us like old acquaintances. When I knocked on the door of the Hanselwanter family,[110] Mrs. Hanselwanter was genuinely glad to see us. When I lamented that I was once again without a roof over my head, she immediately agreed to take us in. She still remembered us fondly. She kept Silvan right then and there, and I went back to Zams to fetch what little luggage I had. Why did I not think of Pettnau sooner? Here people will certainly help us.

Unfortunately, we had to vacate the room at the Hanselwanters' after only a few days. We had to make room for an elderly priest who was well-known here and who had asked for lodging. He was afraid of the bombs in Innsbruck. But Frau Hanselwanter wants to put us up with relatives at the other end of the village. Pettnau stretches lengthwise along a road about 6 kilometers long.

LATE MARCH 1945

We had yet another bad experience. Frau Hanselwanter meant well when she took us to the farmer Kleiner,[111] but he is a cantankerous old curmudgeon, and even though he has a large house and a lot of room, he only reluctantly agreed to host us. He stipulated that no matter what, we had to eat at the Oettl Inn a half hour away. The rich farmer, who is known as a miser, could not even spare something for us in exchange for payment.

When his wife invited us for dinner on our first evening, after all, I observed just how little attention she paid to cleanliness in her cooking. I witnessed how at the end of the meal the family took their used spoons and wiped them on the dirty rag of a tablecloth before they put them back in the drawer from where I, too, had received my spoon. I instantly lost all desire ever to eat anything in this house again and gladly went to the tavern.

It took us three days to discover what was robbing us of our sleep. Our beds were so infested with fleas, we feared being eaten alive. But it was the farmer's treatment of us that proved an even greater incentive for us to leave in a hurry. He treated us as if we were his enemies. What a peculiar man. I am afraid of him. In no other home have I ever observed so much piety. The whole day he and his children could be heard reciting the Hail Mary in such an awful cadence, my ears are still hurting from it. This was simply not normal. Overall, he struck me as a troubled, reclusive man. He takes Holy Communion every day but is unpopular in the village.

We thus knocked on the neighbor's door, a rather poor widow with four well-behaved children. Even though she could spare only a tiny room for us with just one bed, we feel very much at home with Maria Ladner.[112] Silvan and I share the bed.

But things do not look so good for us at the Oettl Inn where we eat every day. Several high-ranking party functionaries and their families are staying in this very well-appointed house, and whenever these gentlemen in their brown uniforms and high boots storm the dining room with roars of "Heil Hitler," I lose my appetite. (One sleazy fellow among them always struts into the room as if he were a pimp. I dislike him the most.)

EARLY APRIL 1945

To make matters worse, an elderly couple from Hamburg tried to make my acquaintance. He is a captain, and both of them wear party insignias. This is turning into a most unpleasant situation for me. I always greet them with "Grüss Gott" and they reply with "Heil Hitler." Then the proprietor, Herr Oettl, himself a committed member of the party, sent the waitress to tell me that he could no longer manage to cook for everyone and we should eat in the home where we were staying. (Of course, members of the party could get anything their hearts desired on this large farm.) I asked Frau Ladner if she would permit me to eat lunch with her in her home. She knows that I am a Jew, and this way I may be able to evade the dangers lurking at Oettl's inn.

Now Frau Ladner's children tell me that the farmer Kleiner has been saying that I am a Jew. The boys, who are quite attached to me, are worried. In particular, they warned me about their teacher who has said that all Jews should be annihilated. For their part, they will not say anything to anyone, so that nothing bad happens to me. They asked me not to go near their school so that the teacher could not see me. He told them that all Jews had black hair and black eyes, and I had both. Their apparent distress made me smile. How their devotion pleases me! But how does the farmer Kleiner know anything about me? Previously, I was only known in lower Pettnau, and I cannot imagine that the good people there would have said anything. I am also sure that Frau Ladner has held her tongue.

The elderly priest finally revealed to me where Kleiner got his information: His wife once asked me where we were from. I responded that I had stayed with the priest in Elbigenalp. The farmer then made inquiries in the village as to why I had to leave the rectory there, and someone told him that I was a Jew. He immediately took this piece of information to the local party leader, the proprietor Oettl, and demanded that he inform the district commissioner in Innsbruck about my stay here.[113] But Oettl refused to report me since I surely had not harmed anyone. Now the farmer Kleiner wants to go to the district commissioner himself. No wonder the proprietor Oettl no longer wants me in his inn.

The elderly priest is most concerned about us.[114]

The children of the village are my greatest joy. Every afternoon ten children (sometimes even more) accompany me to the St. Mary's chapel outside the village where we decided to pray for peace until the bloodshed comes to an end. This is what we vowed to do. The children join in with much enthusiasm. We recite three Our Fathers followed by a hymn to the Virgin Mary before we make our way back to the village together.

In the evening, they visit me to practice new hymns. But the children are never content with just that and I have to play with them. They are impressed that I am the best dodgeball player among them, even though there are older boys in the group. I always had a special talent for ball games, and now I can use it to win the affection of the children in this otherwise cruel era. Whenever I walk through the village, I hear shouts of "Erna, Erna!" from all directions. The children address me with the informal "you" and only use my Christian name. They know I am their loyal friend. I nonetheless exercise considerable influence over them, both boys and girls, large and small. They listen to me, and I seek to undo some of the damage they suffer at the hands of their Nazi teacher. None of my children are ever absent from morning Mass. They come willingly and out of a great love for Christ. For the afternoon devotion with me, they are present with all their hearts.

At least my time with the children distracts me a little from my overwhelming anxiety about Gustav from whom I have not received any more news. The children fill my whole day. In the morning, I copy sheet music for them or I spend time with the youngest children. Directly after lunch, the older ones swoop in. Whenever any of the children hurt themselves, the task of bandaging the wound naturally falls to me. As I am the mother of a boy, I always keep a small stash of bandages with me. Silvan takes part in everything, especially the singing, which he likes.

The elderly retired priest, Father Baron Bettenburg,[115] takes joy in my devotion to the children, but he is concerned about me and has warned me that I must not let it be known that we pray for peace. I could suffer dire consequences if the party got wind of it because peace at all cost was dishonorable in its eyes. For me, the entire war was an unjust affair, and I explain to the children that some people still did not want peace and if someone should ask, they should say that we were praying for the soldiers. This is what we do after all, although we do not pray that the soldiers continue to obediently submit to their slaughter. Rather, we pray that fathers and brothers can soon return home to their loved ones. May God answer our prayers. The children comprehended quite well what I told them and will not say anything about it. For a long time now, I have trusted children more than adults, and children have yet to disappoint me.

LATE APRIL 1945

The Ladner boys serve at elderly Father Baron Bettenburg's Mass every morning, and they deliver daily messages from him in which he details the latest news from the forbidden foreign broadcasts. I immediately burn the messages; the children are trustworthy. I am in a race with freedom. Will the Americans get here in time? If the county commissioner decides to make a move against me, I could still be lost. My nerves are strained to the breaking point. The waiting is almost unbearable. It is a good thing that I am sufficiently occupied; otherwise I could not bear this uncertainty. I have been unable to sleep at night for quite some time now, as I am haunted by all kinds of worst-case scenarios.

The enemy approaches. The villagers are very fearful and worry a great deal. Because so many SS troops are stationed in the region, they have little hope that the handover will go smoothly. Most houses already have a white flag ready, as do we. But there is the danger of flying the flag too soon, in which case the SS would intervene. It would indeed be a worst-case scenario.

Frau Ladner greatly fears the Americans. I assure her that I speak English and would tell them immediately that I was Jewish and that my child and I found shelter in her home. Then they would certainly leave her in peace.

Over these past few days, retreating German troops have transformed the village into a military encampment, and soldiers have been quartered in our home as well. Frau Ladner and I are afraid of these often feral-looking men. Because there are no adults besides us in the home and the eldest boy is only fifteen years old, we do not let the soldiers spend the night in the house. They have to sleep in the barn. But even this arrangement does not alleviate all my fears since my room can be accessed from the barn. I always make sure to tightly lock the door at night. We also cook for the soldiers. Overall, they are in low spirits; but even now, there are still Hitler enthusiasts among them. Whenever someone asks me a question, I am honest and say that I am a Jew hoping for liberation. Sometimes my response sets off heated debates, and at night I am afraid that some of the fanatics might take vengeance on my boy and me for the lost war.

Other than that, we lead a quite idyllic yet fairly primitive life here in Pettnau. In the morning we wash at the well outside the house, even in the cold. Cleanliness is a must in my book! Sporting only his swim trunks on these occasions, Silvan is not always so enthused when I thoroughly douse him in cold water. At table we eat with everyone else from one bowl. On our first day Frau Ladner gave us plates but Silvan pushed his aside and declared: "No, I am eating from the bowl together with the children." Even though I did not find the adjustment quite as easy, after that day I also gave up my plate.

The Ladner boys have erected a shelter halfway up the large hill that rises quite steeply directly behind the house. There is a large military presence in the village and in case there is a battle, we will take refuge there. Silvan and I helped, dragging boards and tools up the hill. We camouflaged the hut with branches and took up some food, but I hope we will not have to make use of the hut.

The military has left, but it is rumored that a large contingent of SS troops is lying in wait on the other side of the river, almost directly across from us.

MAY 5, 1945

It is almost unbelievable. We have survived the war. Everything went well. Not a single shot was fired. Even though for me it truly meant release from mortal danger, I cannot quite share people's jubilation. I keep silent and to myself, and I do not want to see any soldiers. I do not like soldiers. Blood clings to their hands, and in this case it is the blood of my countrymen.[116]

LATE MAY 1945

Now we really have peace and for me this means true freedom. But I cannot be happy about it. How small-minded people are! These members of the master race, who had deemed everyone else unworthy and who despised, derided, and hated me, now grovel for my friendship. This is harder to bear than their malice. For fear that the Americans might hold them accountable they now claim that they never harbored any enmity against Jews (and yet I often enough felt the brunt of it). These people are too pathetic for me to dirty my hands on them. Neither the district commissioner of Reutte, who persecuted me to the end, nor the "pious" Herr Kleiner, nor the "courageous" priest of Bschlabe, nor the district party treasurer, who so often showed his contempt for me, have anything to fear from me. Indeed, after the local party leader Oettl asked me to, I even attested that he had left me in peace.[117] I did it because, when the Americans arrested him, he was so afraid I almost felt ashamed for him. What I said was true but his wife was always quite vicious toward me. But now she has forgotten everything and flatters me to no end. I find it unbearable. The farmer Kleiner has been avoiding me, and I want him to fear me a little. In fact, I wish it upon him with all my heart. After all, I had to live in fear of him for a long time. And my fear was justified! The important gentlemen from the Oettl Inn have been taken away and imprisoned along with the proprietor Oettl.

The captain from Hamburg and his wife both attempted suicide. The woman escaped with her life but he succumbed to his wounds. The incident caused a great commotion in the village. The villagers did not want the man to be buried in the church cemetery, not just because he had committed suicide but mainly because he was not from the town and a Nazi. But when the priest told me that the captain made a most penitent confession and received the last rites,[118] I appealed to the farmers' conscience; they now follow everything I have to say. I told them that if God had forgiven the captain, they, in good conscience, could too. He was buried in the local cemetery, and because none of the farmers wanted to take part in the burial, I once again called on the children. Together we wove funeral wreaths and prayed at the open casket (I told the children that we must forgive people). We also attended the burial. For the widow our presence was a consolation but she had trouble comprehending why I was willing to help her. But if people continue to hate, how can there ever truly be peace?

Otherwise I can hardly bear to be among people and I keep to myself. The children alone receive all of my love. When the war came to an end, the children came to me and said that God had heard our daily prayers in the chapel outside of the village. We still sing together quite often, and on occasion even during Mass in church. The grumbling among some farmers that the village's youth were now taking center stage in church leaves me cold. The children participate with more eagerness, love, and enthusiasm than the adults could ever muster.

The Americans had barely set foot in the village when Silvan came down in the night with a high fever and sore throat. I became quite worried when I learned the next morning that an adult in the village had died from diphtheria that night. Since I did not have a travel permit, I hoped via a passing bicyclist to send a message to the doctor in Telfs, 5 kilometers away. But my worries grew when no one had come by midday. Since the road was clogged with military vehicles, I flagged down an American car, and as coincidence would have it, an American chaplain was inside. In response to my plea delivered in poor English, he promised to send a doctor right away. He returned after only a quarter of an hour. Unfortunately, the German doctor was not at home and he asked me if he could bring over an American physician. At that moment all the bitterness of my past experiences burst out of me, and I told the chaplain that I was of Jewish descent and had not been permitted to call on a physician for the past ten years. I recalled an incident in Berlin from years ago: An injury on my finger forced me to seek out a surgeon in the neighborhood. Because I had to assume that he knew of me, I was obligated to tell him that I was a Jew and asked him whether he would treat me. He felt compelled to phone the local medical board to inquire whether he could take me on as a patient. He returned with the message that he had not received permission to treat me and therefore could not help me. Despite the throbbing pain, he sent me away. Thus I told the chaplain that I no longer had any faith in German physicians and asked him to send an American doctor to me. He immediately drove back to Telfs, but because no one was there, he returned with the suggestion to securely wrap the boy in blankets. We would take him to a Jewish doctor, a US captain, stationed 10 kilometers up the river. This is how I made the acquaintance of Dr. Lampert,[119] a fellow German born in Bonn and a typical Rhinelander. He told me that in 1936 he made the heartwrenching decision to leave Germany to finish medical school in America since Jewish students had been barred from German universities. He had hoped to find his parents and siblings on his return. He did travel to the Rhineland but he made the journey in vain as he was unable to find any of his loved ones. He has given up all hope of finding even one of his many relatives alive, since all traces point to the infamous gas chambers in Poland. Those were the "resettlement camps." I am gripped by fear for my brother and my other Jewish relatives. What has happened to them?

The doctor vaccinated Silvan and took a swab. Luckily, my fear of diphtheria was unfounded. But for a few days he still had a high fever, and every day Dr. Lampert drove up in his jeep to look after him. Even now as the boy is doing better, he still visits us almost every day. He has become a good and supportive friend to me, and he is the first person in some time to whom I have become close.

Now that Silvan is out of danger, I am once again overwhelmed by my worries for Gustav. This cannot continue. I have to do something. I talked it over with Dr. Lampert, and he suggested that I apply for a travel permit from the Americans in Telfs and use it to travel to the military government in Innsbruck. Perhaps they could do something for me there. I got a permit today, but only after a lot of effort because all civilian travel is still prohibited. Tomorrow I plan to go to Innsbruck. It is impossible for me to walk the 20 kilometers to the city on foot since for some time now I have experienced bouts of paralysis in my left leg while walking. Because there are no trains or buses running, there is only one way to get there, namely, by flagging down an American car, like a vagabond, and asking for a ride. I will take my boy for protection, and I am sure all will go well.

JUNE 1945

In Innsbruck the Americans almost interned us in a camp. Refusing to accept my travel permit from Telfs, they demanded to know why I had left my place of residence, which is forbidden. I was most upset and asked for an interpreter, so that I could communicate my thoughts more clearly. I simply do not know enough English for a good rant since I did not learn the correct vocabulary for it in school. Once they realized in the office how worried I was about Gustav, they made note of everything I knew about him with the promise to investigate and send a message to me in Pettnau. Afterward they sent me to an officers' mess hall because one of the Americans was to drive us back home. But since it was already evening and the officer apparently did not feel like driving into the Oberinntal that late in the day, he took us to a hotel next door. He told us to be ready at eight the next morning, when he would drive us back. It was a good thing that I had Silvan with me or I would have been afraid of the many soldiers there as the hotel was mostly reserved for Americans. The next day we arrived safely back in Pettnau.

A few days ago Silvan and I visited Bishop Paulus who is currently staying in Mötz. (It is just a few train stations from here.) As always, he was gracious and attentive to us. The bishop is one of the few people whom I trust.

JULY 1945

Recently three Jewish American soldiers drove up to our farm to talk with me. They told me that they had learned that a Jewish woman lived here from the chauffeur of the American chaplain, who had overheard our conversation in English. I became pretty suspicious because I had heard that a group of Americans were frequent guests at a house in Unterpettnau where they made merry, and I thought that these Jewish soldiers wanted to do the same here. For this reason, I was rather wary when I asked them what they wanted, and their leader, an officer, asked to speak to me briefly in private. (The whole family was outside with me and looked on in amazement.) I saw no other option but to ask him to step inside the house. He was very kind to us. He asked whether we lacked anything and pressed me to accept chocolate and cookies for Silvan. This is how I made the acquaintance of Dr. Wolf from Hamburg who had studied music in Vienna and later fled with his parents to America. He is a refined and tactful man. We get along very well, and he spends all his free time with us. He serves as an interpreter in the military government. Silvan has become his special friend, and recently Dr. Wolf said that one day he wanted to have a son who looked and talked just like my boy. Spoiling him more than I like, he fulfilled Silvan's fondest wish when he gave him an American soldier's helmet. Silvan plays with it all day long. I cannot stand it since truly there has been enough "playing" at being soldiers already. I was therefore quite pleased when an American ripped the helmet from his head during a parade because Silvan most eagerly saluted along with the soldiers as he watched from the sidelines. Silvan cried uncontrollably and keeps nagging Dr. Wolf to get him a new one, but I will not hear of it.

I have been staying with the Sisters of Mercy near the Kettenbrücke in Innsbruck these past few days. Dr. Wolf noticed my difficulties walking and advised me to seek medical treatment. Then he saw our primitive living quarters—a storage chamber filled to the brim with old household goods and furnished with a straw mattress—and without my knowledge he sought out Bishop Paulus and asked him to arrange for a Catholic nursing home in Innsbruck to take me in. It is easier for me to search for Gustav from here. I never received word from the military government, and with my ailing leg I make my way as best I can from one office to the next. I file search requests and follow official proclamations. But so far my efforts have been in vain. Dr. Luterotti oversees my medical treatment, but there is little he can do for me since he is a surgeon.

In Dr. Luterotti's clinic I met the Danish Protestant convert Dr. Wulf. We talked a lot about religious matters, and once he noticed my considerable doubts, he took me to his friend Dr. Huber, a very religious man. Since then, the three of us have met often to talk about our problems. I sense that I am beginning to find my way back to humanity. Just think how far I have stood apart from others these past few years. It will be a long time before I can overcome my feelings of being an outcast. Together with the musician, Dr. Wolf, these two genuinely good men try their best to make me forget all of the pain and misery of the past years. But will I ever be able to forget?

Dr. Wolf conducted his first concert in Innsbruck. Beethoven. He invited me since he knows how much I love music. For the first time in ten years I set foot inside a concert hall and mixed with other people. Musically, it was a great and wonderful experience, but the people surrounding me almost proved my undoing. I can no longer bear them, and had Dr. Wulf and Dr. Huber not attended to me and tried to restore my equanimity with their loving devotion, the experience would have overwhelmed me.

That evening Dr. Wolf, the conductor, was showered with flowers, which he sent to me the next day. I used the flowers to decorate Our Lady's Chapel, and he was quite pleased when I showed him what I had done with them. He appreciated my intentions even though he is of the Jewish faith.

AUGUST 1945

At the beginning of the month I returned to Pettnau. Because Dr. Wolf did not have time to drive me back in his car, we rode in a truck that was serving for public transportation in the Oberinntal. Shortly before our departure a very squalid-looking man climbed in and was greeted with enthusiasm by some people. The commotion drew my attention to him, and I heard him say that he came from a forced-labor camp in Thüringen. I immediately turned to him and told him that my husband, too, had been interned in a forced-labor camp in Thüringen because I was a Jew and that I had not heard from him in a long time. He replied that he was half-Jewish and was imprisoned in a camp near Halle. But he knew nothing about Gustav. He was manager for the Schindler company in Telfs, and he apologized for his shabby appearance, which clearly embarrassed him even though it really was not his fault. As we continued our conversation, I told him that we were quite deserted and alone. We were certain to run out of money soon and after that I knew of no way forward. Even though we had a very kind uncle in Zurich who would surely be willing to take us in for a while, I had no way to get in touch with him. In response the gentleman suggested that I come to Telfs where he would introduce me to Dr. Schindler, who was Swiss and who would certainly be willing to help me.

Two days later I went to Telfs, where Dr. Schindler readily agreed to help me. He intended to travel to Switzerland in the coming days and planned on making a detour to Zurich. Dr. Schindler knew of Uncle Kofmehl,[120] since my uncle is a well-known personality in Switzerland. Dr. Schindler will tell him about us and send word upon his return.

EARLY AUGUST 1945

We are in dire need of a few things from Tannheim because, for almost three quarters of a year, we have made do with the things I was able to stuff into a rucksack. As we made our way to Tannheim on a truck, we drove over the Fernpass and saw that the hotel from which we had been so rudely expelled this past winter had burned down to its foundation. The entire area gave off an eerie impression of devastation, and taking in this sight we could not quite suppress a feeling of satisfaction. The fighting between the SS and the Americans here had been fierce and many had died. From the truck we indeed saw numerous burial mounds. They had been so concerned for their own safety, but in the end they did not escape their fate.

Our friends in Tannheim rejoiced upon our return, but to my sorrow and against all my expectations, no mail from Gustav awaited me there. Normal postal services have not yet resumed but I thought that perhaps he would find a way to send me a message.

As always, we stayed with Michl and Sefa. We owe our deepest gratitude to these two dear human beings. Even though they had to endure many hardships on our account, they always stayed true to us. They share my fears for Gustav, and every day after meals they pray the Lord's Prayer for his safe return.

The village has become quiet. The out-of-towners are all gone; the mayor has received his just punishment. I can now walk about without fear, and Silvan and I visit everyone who stood by us in hard times. But first and foremost we visit the grave of good Frau Binosa.

I yearn to return to the Inntal. Dr. Wolf will soon leave Tyrol with the remaining remnant of American troops since the French have taken over the region's occupation, and I want to say farewell to him; Dr. Lampert already left a few weeks ago. I am also hoping to find a message from Uncle Emil in Telfs.

EARLY SEPTEMBER 1945

We are back in Pettnau. Uncle Emil asked Dr. Schindler to give me 1,000 marks in his name. I am to let him know when I need more money, and he wants us both to join him until we can find Gustav. My uncle and aunt are most concerned about us and want to help. I must now try to obtain visas. Dr. Schindler advised us to travel to the nearest consulate in Bregenz; he said it was the quickest way to take care of everything.

I find it difficult once again to travel into the unknown but it seems I have no choice. But how will Gustav find us? He probably thinks that we are in Tannheim. On the other hand, we once agreed in Berlin that if we lost each other in Germany we would meet up at his relatives' place in Zurich. Perhaps he remembers our conversation. We once again move on. We who have become homeless are nowhere at home anymore. It does not matter where we eke out our existence.

OCTOBER 1945

Tired and shattered, I am resting in a sanatorium in Mehrerau. Things in Bregenz turned out to be much more difficult than I had anticipated. When I left Pettnau four weeks ago, the proprietor Oettl gave me a letter of recommendation for the guest master at Mehrerau Abbey near Bregenz.[121] (He went to school there years ago.) He feared that I might not find lodging for Silvan and me in Bregenz even for a few days until I could take care of everything at the consulate. He therefore instructed me to turn to the abbey where they could surely help me. We arrived in Bregenz in the afternoon and asked in vain for a room at various hotels. It was already getting dark and fearing to be left without shelter, I went to Mehrerau. Walking has become increasingly difficult for me, and I arrived in a state of exhaustion. The abbey is still largely occupied by laypersons because the Nazis had confiscated it, and the monks (Cistercians) are only gradually moving back in. The guest master was not eager to take in more strangers, but he nonetheless gave my boy and me a room. Later I had to speak to the steward, whom I told that I was waiting for a Swiss visa so that I could join my relatives. He replied that this could take a while. I could stay for two days but then I had to move on. That night in the bare cell I could not sleep because I sensed that we were not welcome here, and I vowed to spend the next night outside with my child rather than remain here as an intruder. Hence, the next morning I immediately went to the steward, paid what I owed, and told him that I was moving on.

Feeling quite helpless, we wandered through the small city. Even though in the past I often did not know where I would spend the night with my boy, I was now gripped by an unspeakable fear of the days ahead. This unfamiliar place depressed me terribly. As we were passing by the Sacred Heart Church, Silvan and I entered it in the hope of finding some solace. As we were leaving the church, we chanced upon a priest at the entrance and because he greeted us in the friendliest manner I asked to speak with him. I shared the most pressing facts about our situation and asked whether he knew of a family that would be willing to let us a room for a few days. Eager to help, Father Schöch invited us to stay in his own house since his guestroom happened to be empty.[122] It was not the fault of this exemplary, gracious priest that troubled days lay ahead of me.

Getting hold of the necessary papers has proved very difficult. I have been sent from one office to the next, so far without any success. Then after fourteen days of relentless worrying and problems I fell ill. I spent a few days in bed in Father Schöch's house (I simply could no longer walk) before he arranged for me to be admitted to the Mehrerau sanatorium.[123] But what am I to do now? I do not know anyone in this cold, industrious city. Uncle Emil keeps writing to me to obtain the necessary exit permits while he is trying to get entry visas from Zurich. He says he can probably get one for Silvan, but for me there will inevitably be more difficulties.

Perhaps it is better for me to remain in Austria because I must do everything I can to find Gustav. He probably thinks I am in Tyrol; it will be easier for us to meet up here. My worries about him exhaust me.

Although I have not yet forgotten my unfriendly reception at the abbey, I did speak with a priest from Mehrerau today who currently ministers to the sick here. Even though I believe he has my best interest at heart, I cannot quite trust strangers yet. Since the persecution has ceased, an all-consuming disquiet has been raging inside of me. Now that I no longer have anything to fear from mankind, I feel less at home in the world than in times of danger. Then there is my complete physical exhaustion. The priest invited me to pay him a visit in the abbey once I have recovered a bit, in order to speak to him about my worries. Here in the sanatorium he has to minister to many patients, which leaves little time for any one individual. Should I return to the abbey, even though I have already had a painful experience there? Whenever Father Paul is in the sanatorium he comes to my room.[124] He is unfailingly friendly, even though I am not particularly welcoming and responsive.

I guess there is no point dwelling on all the bitterness that lies behind me. Once and for all, I should draw a line under the past and begin anew. But at this point it is still nearly impossible because first I must find out what happened to all of my relatives. From everything I hear, most of them are probably dead.

No news of Gustav has arrived yet. Is he, at least, alive? My hope is no longer great. I just received word from Brussels that my brother Max was carried off to Poland, where it is said he perished in the gas chambers.[125] His wife is inconsolable. She knows neither the place nor the date of his death. Only gradually do I learn about the entire gruesome nature of the Nazi regime. It is only now that I realize the constant danger I was in these past years. A few days ago I went to a Jewish Committee Office at the Kornmarkt where I learned that almost everyone interned in the transit camp in the Grosse Hamburger Strasse in Berlin was later carried off to the gas chambers in Poland. They told me how extraordinary it was that I escaped this camp unharmed, and that I must give up any hope of finding Grete Merzbach and her family alive since the influential and well-known family Merzbach was completely annihilated.[126] There was also little hope that my brother or any of my relatives from Cologne were still alive.

Dear God, I cannot bear being the only survivor of my large family in Germany. Once I am certain that Gustav is dead, then I do not want to go on living. Nor do I want to let my child live. What are we to do here? We are completely alone and, truth be told, most people still despise us. I will do my boy a service if I spare him the fate of becoming a man who does not have a home anywhere on earth.

NOVEMBER 1945

We have found a path forward for Silvan. Uncle Emil was able to obtain an entry permit for the boy, and Silvan has been in Zurich for several days already. I know that he is in good and caring hands. But my own life is now completely worthless. For as long as I had to fight for the preservation of my child my life had purpose but this is no longer the case. I am standing before a great void. Even God can no longer help me. For some time I have had the feeling that the life I am living now is completely disconnected from the past. It is as if I had died in the meantime and reemerged on earth under completely different circumstances. This is how foreign the world I live in now seems to me. I am unable to overcome the loss of almost all of my relatives, and I am pained by the space that inexorably separates me from the other people to whom I was once close.

I visited Father Paul at the abbey. I am certain now that he means well. I am in need of someone to help me, and I will have to get used to his rough and sober demeanor. There is something about him that makes me feel safe in his presence. He values my Jewishness and told me that my ancestry did not stand in contradiction to my Christian faith. On the contrary, he calls Christianity the consistent fulfillment of Judaism. He told me that for over twenty years he has been a member of a league of Catholic priests who fight for the rights of Jews.[127] On account of this fact alone I feel I can confide in him. As a convert, I asked him for additional education in the Catholic faith so that I could deepen my inadequate knowledge.

However, the most important thing at the moment is that Father Paul wants to assist me in my search for Gustav. I gave him two letters addressed to Gustav's old address in Halle and to Father Erwin in Berlin. Perhaps the latter knows something about my husband. Father Paul gave the letters to his sister who kindly smuggled them across the border to Germany. Postal services have not yet resumed. I once again have a little hope.

DECEMBER 1945

My life in the sanatorium is pretty bleak. How I long for a kind word. The sisters have no sympathy for me, and sometimes I think I am even sensing outright enmity. I dread Christmas without Gustav and Silvan. I have never been so alone. Father Paul means well but with his somewhat coarse Bavarian manner he does not quite find the right tone. In spite of my difficulties walking and the uninviting, gloomy weather, I walk for many hours every day along the lake, which looms gray and threatening before me, or in the nearby forest, which looks almost as dreary as the trampled, bleak pine forests in Berlin. I must fight this devastating despair and have patience. The uncertainty about Gustav's fate is harder to bear than any gruesome reality. All this futile hoping and waiting. Maybe he is still alive; maybe I will find him. Maybe! Nothing is certain anymore, and I cling to any remote possibility [that he may be alive].

I will spend Christmas in Höchst with a woman who has four grown daughters. I met the woman by chance, and she invited me. She thinks it will be easier for me to bear the loneliness in a family rather than here in the sanatorium. I have accepted the invitation to distract myself. My uncle and aunt from Zurich write warm letters to me. Silvan is doing well, and they hope that I find Gustav soon. They also sent me a little Christmas package.

EARLY JANUARY 1946

Gustav lives! I received a message from him. On St. Stephen's Day a priest from Mehrerau brought a postcard from him to Höchst, which reached me through Michl in Tannheim. He is still in a makeshift hospital in Halle. Thank God, certainty at last. Maybe my own letter has reached him in the meantime? He must worry about us.

I did not expect Father Paul to turn out to be such a kind and helpful person. In an effort to distract me a little from my worries, he gave me a small assignment. At the moment, there is an exhibition in the parish hall of the Abbey titled "Christian Home Design," to which Father Paul contributed his own beautiful wood carvings. I am supervising the exhibition for the next eight days, which is a welcome diversion. In particular I like a holy water font carved by Father Paul so much that I frequently pause before it. Christ is depicted in low relief at the Jacob's well and next to him stands the Samaritan woman. Lord, still my thirst by the living waters. A pump handle rises from the well on which hangs the font, a little bucket, for the holy water. Father Paul noticed the joy I took in it. Was it presumptuous of me to ask him to give it to me? I am grateful that I am even permitted to walk among these beautiful pieces of art, but most of all that he had no reservations about employing a Jew for this task.

Father Paul rode his bicycle to Lindau yesterday to pick up the mail that was waiting for me there. He brought me a heartrending letter from Gustav. He writes hurriedly, with pencil and in a state of obvious agitation:

> Dearest Erna,
> I just received word from Father Erwin in Berlin that you had written. He let me know that I could write to you but not where you were. Presumably still in Austria in Pettnau or in Tannheim? [The letter was smuggled across the border and for this reason I could not list my residence.] Since I believed you dead, you can imagine my joy.

I was confined to my bed until the end of September. Since June 22,
I have been wearing a body cast, and at the moment I am on my second
version of it. You must know that an ulceration caused by the thrombo-
sis in my leg has destroyed my first and second vertebrae. This was only
discovered after the fact at the beginning of June through X-rays! At the
moment I can only walk with great difficulty, like an old man. There is
no telling how much longer I have to wear the cast (two years?). Natu-
rally, I am unable to work. The health insurance has stopped payments,
and I live on public assistance. Things will never again be like they were
before. For the entire year I have not been out in the sun and fresh air,
and I have suffered much hunger. I weigh approximately 50 kilograms.
[Gustav is 1.76 meters tall.][128] *You can imagine that recovery requires*
good food, and now the time has come when you can help me. If I have
someone to care for me, there is no need for me to remain in the hospital!
I need to be with you now.

Rumor has it that the Russian border is open at intervals but I can-
not risk a journey on my own in light of the current travel conditions. I
have registered for a group transport to Pettnau in Austria but I doubt
that the Russians will authorize it. If you can't get an entry permit for
me, I don't see a way forward.

If you are in Tannheim, you could perhaps find me a good place in
Pfronten, with the sisters or through the mayor? Berlin is currently off
limits due to food shortages. Our apartment is supposedly still standing.
For eight days the Russians wreaked havoc in it and took all beds and
bed linens with them. Halle too is closed off to newcomers, and there is
little to eat here as well. It is only in the south with you that I could re-
cover. Please help me as best you can. I may travel if my transport south
is authorized because I really want to leave this place and join you. If I
only knew where you were! I will ask Father Erwin. It would be best if we
never again had to return to Berlin. Can't you make it happen? Can you
imagine how much I longed for you and the sun this past summer when
I lay prostrate in bed in excruciating pain? I sent letters to Jungholz and
the train station inn in Nesselwang but I have had no word so far. If we
could only be together again but not here only in the country, in the south!

All my love to you and dear Silvan.

Your Gustav

I want to go to him, to help him but Father Paul advises me to be prudent and wait until he can come here and that would only be possible if I remained in Bregenz. Here I could help him, and here he could get badly needed care. Besides, it was questionable if I could even get as far as Halle. The idle waiting is unbearable. What should I do?

JANUARY 17, 1946

Gustav arrived unexpectedly last evening at around ten o'clock. My joy was mixed with bitter pain at his pitiful appearance. I was utterly shocked at the sight of him. Hunger has reduced him to a mere skeleton. Hunched over, he stood before me, his hair grayed and his face marked by countless worries and deprivations. This is what Hitler has turned this healthy, upright, forty-three-year-old man into! Clad in a heavy plaster armor that covered his entire upper body, he had dragged himself here in three days. He took the train for most of the way but still had to cover long stretches on foot. Mentally he is quite broken as well. It is difficult not to start hating! How I torture myself with reproaches! It is because of me that he has become a cripple! Will he recover? Can he be cured? The medical director at the sanatorium will care for him. He has given me hope.

LATE JANUARY 1946

The doctor diagnosed Gustav with skeletal tuberculosis. Two vertebrae in his spine are completely destroyed, and until the healing process culminates in the formation of stable cartilage, he will have to lie in a body cast for years to come. Poor Gustav! But he is strangely resigned to his bitter fate. Life has been extremely hard for him these past few years. He has suffered so many hardships and deprivations. During his months-long hospital stay in a room with seventeen beds, where people constantly came and went, he saw so many suffer and die. But now he feels quite comfortable here. How glad he is to have me back, but he does miss his boy very much, whom he has not seen for almost three years. He is glad, though, that Silvan is in such good hands in Switzerland.

Emotionally, too, Gustav has not been able to come to terms with his time in the camp. Over and over, a dreadful agony pours out of him; how inhumanely they were treated. This is how it began: In Berlin he was assigned to the "Aktion Mitte," where he was joined by many other men married to Jews who, like him, were "race defilers." They had to report in Grunewald,[129] where a fat OT man on a perch behind barbed wire sarcastically called out everyone's name. At night, they set out from there into the unknown. By train they traveled via Dessau to Weissenfels, where their train was left standing on the freight tracks for twelve hours. The train personnel were told that the cars contained Jews. At dusk, they were marched through the city in tight formation and quartered in a damp cellar somewhere. Later they were moved to the attic of a giant labor camp. Foreigners were used to guard them. The foreigners were deemed more trustworthy than the regular guards. At first they were used for excavation work and the loading and unloading of materials at the bunker construction site near the Leunawerke.[130] As second-class human beings they were not permitted to work in the factory itself. About 30,000 people worked in the ruins of the already heavily damaged Leunawerke. At 4:00 a.m. every day they were driven 15 kilometers from Weisenfels to Leuna, and then they had to march in designated groups and under heavy guard through the factory compound to their workplaces. In the evening they left them to stand for hours on end at the train station in the cold. They worked alongside foreign forced laborers. Gustav was later transferred to a transit camp for foreigners in Halle an der Saale. Their living quarters were furnished only with bare pallets. Here they were employed in rough foundation work as well as in construction and rubble-clearing work. Because he was not used to physical labor, the carrying of heavy iron bars, the loading and unloading of large machinery, and especially the work at a cement-mixing machine proved very difficult for Gustav. They also had to work the nightshift quite often. In their inadequate clothing, they worked in the bitter cold until the air-raid alarm sounded (which happened often), at which point they were penned in a small, overheated barrack. He found this even harder to bear. After the all-clear signal was given, they resumed their work in the cold. The hygienic conditions were indescribable. He often could not wash himself for weeks since forty barracks had to share one washing facility. Gustav could not withstand the exertions in the camp for long, and he fell ill. At first an abscess formed in the sole of his foot, and they took him to the OT's infirmary. After he collapsed in the air-raid protection trench, they put him in a separate room in the attic where he was laid up for two months in temperatures below the freezing point. He could never even get out of his clothes. Despite his illness, they forced him to use the rear staircase during every alarm to get to an ancillary cellar because the main cellar was reserved only for officers, who could not be burdened with the sight of Jews. My husband is a blond Aryan but he had a Jewish wife, which placed him on par with Jews.

When his condition worsened (toward the end of the war) they took him to the university clinic in Halle. Due to frequent air raids, he spent most of his time there in the cellar. Then the building was bombed and he was transferred to a school that had been converted into a makeshift hospital. Because of the terrible pain, he was on morphine for three months before they determined that two of his vertebrae had been destroyed. For a quarter of a year he lay in bed in a plaster body cast before he mustered all his energy and managed to drag himself to Bregrenz. Now he is resting here. He is miserable and ill and always has a high fever. But he is nonetheless overjoyed that he can once again see the sun around noontime every day when it brightly shines down from the wintery sky into his comfortable room.

[1950]

Meanwhile, more than four years have passed, hard, bitterly hard years. This is 1950, the Holy Year. Finally, there is light amid the darkness. Gustav is on the way to recovery. For two years he lay immobilized in a plaster cast. Then he was transferred to the High Alps, and now he can once again walk upright. The X-rays show a complete cartilaginification of the vertebrae.[131]

It was not easy for me to find my bearings amid this turmoil and despair, and it is only because of the kind and wise guidance of Father Paul that I can face our fate with serenity and calmness. But not all the hours I spent with him were edifying ones for me. With unrelenting severity and iron constancy, he demanded that I continue to practice my Christian faith without question. He never once accepted half measures. But my experiences from my time of persecution continue to weigh on me.

Gustav has not been able to fully come to terms with his fate. He is a bitter person, never at peace. Will he ever find his way back to Christianity and through it find inner peace? For two years Gustav was confined to bed in a plaster cast, helpless and lonely. Yet, all that time, Father Paul looked after him in a most devoted manner. But his soul remained unresponsive. His subsequent stay in the High Alps brought him physical healing but he never again became joyful. Perhaps time will help him heal. Once he returns to work, once he rejoins human society, and once his child and I are with him again, then his life will be good once more.

God has held His benevolent hand over our child. The years of persecution did not harm him either physically or mentally. He is a healthy and happy boy. Only the fact that we have been constantly separated these past four years weighs him down since he idolizes his parents. But he also knows that there are limits to this idolization. Recently, he wrote in an essay titled "My Mother" that even though his mother sometimes punishes him—she only does it when he deserves it—she is still the dearest thing in the world to him. But when he read it to me he suddenly exclaimed: "Mama, no, I must not say such things. Do not be angry with me. You are the dearest thing to me on earth, but the dearest to me in the world must be God."

Silvan is now a student of the Jesuits at the Stella Matutina in Feldkirch (Austria).[132] For three-quarters of a year he was in Zurich, where our relatives lovingly cared for his physical and mental well-being. He then attended the village school in Langen near Bregenz for one and a half years, living there with a farming family. There he spent more time in the stables and in the fields than in the classroom and at his studies. He took great joy in farming life and once said to me: "I don't want to attend university. I want to be a farmer. University-educated people are superfluous, unlike the farmers without whom we would have no bread to eat." But later the family tradition broke through, and he has taken to his books with enthusiasm.

Two years ago Father Paul administered First Holy Communion to Silvan right here in the sanatorium's chapel. Father Paul prepared him for this day with much care and devotion, which is the reason that the boy now clings to "Uncle Paul" with all his heart. Only recently he said to me: "Mama, Uncle Paul is a saint, isn't he?" I replied: "Yes, that is quite possible," and he continued: "Mama, really, Uncle Paul is a saint and once he dies we absolutely must get our hands on one of his bones."[133] At the moment we are glad, however, that "Uncle Paul" is still alive because what would we do without him? He seeks to support all three of us and lovingly helps us carry all of our burdens. I look up to him in awe. When I am in his presence, I am able to conquer my fears of the future. He permits me to bring all my worries and fears to him time and again. In this otherwise egotistical era, he is a person who lives entirely to serve others. It is thanks to him that I was able to reemerge into the light from the terrible darkness into which persecution and misery had plunged me. Today, I am certain once more that a benevolent God watches over my life. I know that my path to the Church was the right one.

After all, Father Paul has proved to me repeatedly that there is no contradiction between Judaism and Christianity, just as there is none between flower and fruit or between expectation and fulfillment. Being a Christian, he says, means ultimately to fulfill the sacred Jewish inheritance. The dark One and more-God "Elohim," whom Hermann Cohen calls a veritably unsolvable riddle,[134] reveals himself to me in my faith as One God in three persons [Holy Trinity]. Though the Sinai Covenant protects human dignity and human rights,[135] I find it eclipsed by Jesus's Sermon on the Mount, for it confers human rights and dignity even onto the outcast and the oppressed, even lifting him into the divine realm. I see the crudely earthy, bloody, and yet exemplary cult of my ancestors spiritually and sensually glorified and filled with infinite worth. And as I celebrate the liturgy in the abbey church throughout the year, I see with my own eyes how the old is being adorned with the new. There the hearty psalms of the Jews ring out day and night. I know that a good portion of the chorales I hear and that to me embody the pinnacle of sacred music hail back mostly to the Jewish temple hymns. I rediscover my peoples' ancient and sacred symbols in the wine and bread, in the chalice and the lamb, in the liturgical robes, incense, holy water, candles, salt, ash, oil, the washing of hands, and the blessing. In light of these things, I repeatedly ask myself whether a Jew has reason to deny himself such fulfillment of his own religion, which is a religion of longing and anticipation? At the same time, I ask: Is it is permissible for Christians to hate Jews, these ancestors and trailblazers of their faith, only because they are Jews? How happy I am therefore when, as it so often happens, Father Paul, himself the bearer of the name of a Jewish Christian, tells me: "Tomorrow is a day of celebration for you because we once again commemorate one of the great Jews in God's Church." Through his psychologically sensitive teaching style he has managed to help me overcome my difficulties with the Catholic devotion of Mary, which hails back to my upbringing, and foster a spiritual connection with the Mother of God. Today the Salve Regina is my favorite prayer,[136] and whenever I bid farewell to Father Paul it has become our routine to recite the greeting with which ancient Jews honored Judith, the brave conqueror of Holofernes, and which we now use in the Catholic liturgy to celebrate Mary, the crusher of the serpent's head [Genesis 3:15/Revelation 12:1–18]:

> *Tu gloria Jerusalem,*
> *Tu laetitia Israel*
> *tu honorificentia populi nostri!*
> (You, glory of Jerusalem
> You joy of Israel
> You, honor of our people!)

A tyrant trampled millions of people to death under his boot, and today people curse his name. I did not curse him, I, a minor victim of his madness. I never hated because hate does not magnify us. But why do I nonetheless record this memory? First to impress upon mankind that something like it must never happen again. We, too, want to be recognized as human beings, and if you can look upon Jews without any racial conceit, then you have solved half of the Jewish problem. Second, to confirm that I encountered those forces that unyieldingly fought for human rights and dignity only where the Christian teaching—"There is neither Jew nor Greek, there is neither slave nor free person, there is not male and female; for you are all one in Christ Jesus" (Galatians 3:28)—was not mere words but was consciously lived.

MAY 1952

We will leave Germany in fourteen days. Our hopes have not been fulfilled. On March 28, Gustav succumbed to his grave illness. He died in the peace of God in spite of his bitter fate. Father Paul cared for him until the end. We put him to rest in the mountain cemetery above Bregenz.

Now there is nothing to keep us here, and we have gladly accepted my sister's invitation to come to Chile. Because we no longer wanted to burden Gustav's relatives, we are destitute. But Uncle Emil will pay for our passage.

OCTOBER 1954

Thank God we are back in Germany. Despite all the hardships we had to live through in our homeland, we did not find peace overseas, and we praise the day when chance came to our aid and we were able to leave Chile.

We were drawn south in the vicinity of Gustav's grave. Since we are nowhere at home anymore, we are attempting to put down roots in Freiburg im Breisgau, the city in the middle of the Black Forest Mountains. Will we succeed? We must come to rest somewhere at last.

JANUARY 1963

Freiburg has fulfilled my wish. After almost twenty years of wandering, we finally have a home again. I have reintegrated into society, and we believe that we have made friends. During all of these years, Silvan has been a great consolation to me, helping me to overcome the loss of my husband. He has been studying law at university here these past four years and if all goes well, he will take his first state examination this fall.

From time to time I drive to Bregenz to see Father Paul, to whom I owe so much gratitude. I like to spend time in the quiet mountain cemetery at the foot of the Pfander Mountain. Next to the St. Wendelin's chapel, there is a mosaic on Gustav's grave depicting Moses with the bronze snake. It tells me that just as Moses saved Israel from the poisonous bite of the snake, so Christ brought us redemption and salvation through his cross.

NOTES

1. Gustav and Erna lived in Berlin-Treptow within the boundaries of St. Anna Parish (St. Anna Kapelle) in Berlin-Baumschulenweg. Father Max Zimmermann (1896–1962) was the pastor. The Jesuit priest who presided at the Baptism was not assigned to the parish and is not identifiable.
2. Martha Becker, born Sailer (1875–1942).
3. Isabella Kohen, born David (1871–1943).
4. Following the November pogrom in 1938, the Nazis stepped up their persecution of the remaining Jews in Germany. The regime passed a string of new laws and ordinances with the goal of robbing Jews of their remaining property, isolating them even further from non-Jewish Germans, and ultimately forcing their

emigration. Nazi leaders briefly considered confining Jewish Germans in ghettos but dismissed the idea. Instead, they decided to concentrate Jews in so-called "Jew houses" (*Judenhäuser*) scattered throughout German cities, a measure which, according to Security Squad, or SS, general Reinhard Heydrich, would enable the regime to "control the Jew through the watchful eye of the whole population." Working with the Gestapo, local authorities used the April 1939 Law concerning Tenancy Contracts with Jews to evict Jewish tenants from their homes and force them to move into designated "Jew houses." Although Jews could only be evicted after new accommodations in a "Jew house" had been secured, Isabella Kohen's situation suggests that landlords did not always follow these guidelines. See Ute Daub, "Die Stadt Frankfurt macht sich 'judenfrei': Zur Konzentrierung, Verbannung und Ghettoisierung der jüdischen Bevölkerung zwischen 1938 und 1943," in"*Nach der Kristallnacht": Jüdisches Leben und antijüdische Politik in Frankfurt am Main 1938–1945*, ed. Monica Kingreen (Frankfurt: Campus, 1999), 319–356, here 326.

5. The Daughters of Charity of St. Vincent de Paul are a Catholic women's religious congregation originally dedicated to the nursing of the sick. From 1933 to 1989, the sisters maintained a small house with four sisters in Frankfurt-Eschenheim. The congregation's archives contain no written records of Isabella Kohen's stay in Eschenheim in 1939, but according to the congregation's oral tradition, the sisters secretly housed a number of people persecuted by the Nazi regime.

6. Since the 1920s, the Catholic women's religious congregation of the Grey Sisters of St. Elizabeth (Graue Schwestern von der heiligen Elisabeth) maintained a rest home in Berlin-Schlachtensee where the sisters regularly welcomed guests. Unfortunately, no guest lists have survived from that time. In 1968, the congregation changed its name to Sisters of St. Elizabeth (Schwestern von der heiligen Elisabeth). The editors thank Johannes Mertens of the Provinzarchiv, Kongregation der Schwestern von der heiligen Elisabeth, Provinz Deutschland, for this information.

7. Established in October 1931, the National Socialist German Women's League, or NSF (NS-Frauenschaft), was the only officially recognized women's organization within the National Socialist German Workers' Party that afforded women the opportunity to participate in the Nazi movement. Its 2.3 million members had to attend at least one NSF meeting per month, where ideological schooling focused on women as mothers and wives. Like all Nazi organizations, the NSF adhered to the hierarchical leadership principle (*Führerprinzip*). At the head of the NSF stood the Reich women's leader Gertrud Scholtz-Klink (1902–1999), but women throughout Germany could assume leadership positions on various levels, including the lowest levels of cell or block leaders. Most likely, Erna is referring to one of these lower-ranking NSF leaders responsible for her neighborhood. See Matthew Stibbe, *Women in the Third Reich* (London: Arnold/Oxford University Press, 2003), 34–57.

8. Father Erwin Röhr, O.P. (1907–1977), a Dominican, lived in the Dominican priory adjacent to St. Paul's parish (St. Paulus) in Berlin-Moabit. Following the removal of all Jewish students, including Christians of Jewish heritage, from

German schools, the diocese of Berlin through its Relief Agency of the Berlin Chancery (Hilfswerk beim Bischöflichen Ordinariat Berlin), together with the Protestant-sponsored Office of Pastor Grüber (Büro Pfarrer Grüber), on January 6, 1939, established the Family School on Oranienburger Strasse (Familienschule Oranienburger Strasse), a school for Christian children of Jewish heritage. Father Röhr and his colleagues, Father Raymund Harwardt, O.P. (1901–1982), and Sister Maria Servatie, S.N.D., a member of the Sisters of Notre Dame (Schwestern Unserer Lieben Frau), taught religious education to the Catholic children enrolled there. Other Dominicans from St. Paul's priory also assisted with the teaching until the school's closure on June 30, 1942, following the Reich Minister for Education's decree ordering the transfer of all Jewish students to Jewish schools. Father Röhr and other Dominicans continued to offer religious education secretly in the priory. See Rainer Maria Groothuis, *Im Dienste einer überstaatlichen Macht: Die deutschen Dominikaner unter der NS-Diktatur* (Münster: Regensberg, 2002), 440–441; and Jana Leichsenring, *Die katholische Kirche und "ihre Juden": Das "Hilfswerk beim bischöflichen Ordinariat Berlin" 1938–1945* (Berlin: Metropol, 2007), 169–175.

9. The Catholic Church celebrates the culmination of the liturgical year as one day lasting from Holy Thursday through Easter Sunday evening. The Triduum consists of three liturgies: Mass of the Last Supper, Good Friday of the Lord's Passion, and Mass of the Resurrection of the Lord. See "Triduum," United States Conference of Catholic Bishops, http://www.usccb.org/prayer-and-worship/liturgical-year/triduum/.

10. On the night of November 9, 1938, *Kristallnacht*, or the "Night of Broken Glass," the situation for Jews would change drastically in Germany as SA and SS men in plainclothes along with ordinary Germans brutally destroyed Jewish-owned businesses, homes, and synagogues while terrorizing the German Jewish population in general, murdering over 100 German Jews, destroying more than 190 synagogues, and subsequently arresting and imprisoning more than 30,000 Jews in Dachau, Buchenwald, and Sachsenhausen. The German state followed this action with a series of laws that further removed Jews from German society, especially its professional and economic life. See Alan Steinweis, *Kristallnacht 1938* (Cambridge, MA: Harvard University Press, 2009).

11. Father Walter Krawinkel, Or. (1906–1976) was a priest of the Oratorium of St. Philip Neri whose central house in Germany is in Leipzig. He was pastor (*Kuratus*) of St. Francis Xavier parish (St. Franziskus Xaverius) in Berlin-Baumschulenweg. There is no record of Father Krawinkel having conflicts with state authorities.

12. Beginning in the spring of 1940, German labor offices, in collaboration with private and public enterprises, compelled all able-bodied Jewish Germans to perform forced labor. Even prior to 1940, Jewish forced labor in Germany became commonplace, when in December 1938, the state began to force Jews who received unemployment benefits to perform manual labor in construction or municipal service jobs such as garbage collection. The state interned many of these Jewish

forced laborers in one of at least forty new forced labor camps set up between 1939 and 1941 throughout Germany. While it remains unclear whether Erna's cousins were imprisoned in one of the new forced labor camps or within the separate concentration camp system, it is clear that on the eve of the Holocaust, the increased internment of Jews in both camp systems hastened their social death, as Jews began to "disappear" even prior to the start of large-scale deportations from Germany. See Wolf Gruner, *Jewish Forced Labor under the Nazis: Economic Needs and Racial Aims, 1938–1944* (Cambridge: Cambridge University Press, 2006), 34–37.

13. As a young child, Silvan had listened to the Latin prayers recited at Mass and other liturgies and focused on two Latin words: *homo* (man) and *deus* (God). For Catholics, Jesus Christ is God made flesh, fully human and fully divine. However, no specific prayer begins with these two words, hence, Erna's comment, "We do not know where he learned this phrase."

14. The Second World War commenced on September 1, 1939, with Germany's invasion of Poland. Although both England and France declared war on Germany in September 1939, little fighting took place on the Western front until the commencement of Germany's Western offensive in May 1940. Following the occupation of Denmark and Norway, German troops invaded and quickly defeated neutral Belgium, Luxembourg, the Netherlands, and France. With Belgium's surrender on May 28, 1940, Erna's brother, Max Kohen, and his wife, son, and mother found themselves once again under the authority of Nazi Germany. Max and Isabella Kohen were among the approximately 65,000 to 70,000 Jews who lived in Belgium at the time, most of whom were foreign and stateless Jews, primarily from Poland. Within days of the German invasion, Belgian authorities rounded up and deported the majority of male refugees from Nazi Germany, most of whom were Jewish, to France. Max Kohen was among these deportees while his mother, Isabella, his wife, Martha, and their son, Heinz, remained in Belgium. See the introduction for further information on Max Kohen.

15. The bombing war was a key strategy of the Allies during World War II, and Berlin as the capital of Germany eventually became a major target. Following the commencement of war in the West in the spring of 1940, the British Royal Airforce (RAF) flew its first raid over Berlin on August 25, 1940. The RAF's bombings of Germany in 1940 and 1941 aimed "to bring war back to the German people and so create a possible social and political crisis on the home front." But these early bombings proved fairly ineffective and casualties in Berlin remained relatively low. All in all, Berliners spent about 120 hours in air-raid shelters in 1940, and 222 residents died in the bombings that year. See Richard Overy, *The Bombers and the Bombed: Allied Air Wars over Europe 1940–1945* (New York: Viking, 2013), 12; and Laurenz Demps, "Berlin im Bombenkrieg," in *Berlin 1933–1945*, ed. Michael Wildt and Christoph Kreutzmüller (Munich: Siedler, 2013), 357.

16. In September 1940, the police president of Berlin decreed that houses with both Jewish and non-Jewish residents had to establish separate air-raid shelters for Jewish residents. However, the decree did not apply to Jews in privileged marriages,

and Erna should have been permitted to share the general shelter. But according to historian Andrea Löw, throughout Germany, the treatment of Jews during air raids varied, depending in large part on the attitude of the respective air-raid wardens, neighbors, and local authorities. Whereas many houses had separate cellars for Jews, it was also not unheard of for Jews and non-Jews to share a shelter. See Joseph Walk, ed., *Das Sonderrecht für die Juden im NS-Staat: Eine Sammlung der gesetzlichen Maßnahmen und Richtlinien—Inhalt und Bedeutung*, 2nd ed. (Heidelberg: C. F. Müller, 1996), 327; Bruno Blau, ed., *Das Ausnahmerecht für die Juden in den europäischen Länder 1933–1945*, vol. 1 (New York: William Kober, 1952), 117; Andrea Löw, ed., *Die Verfolgung und Ermordung der europäischen Juden durch das nationalsozialistische Deutschland*, vol. 3, *Deutsches Reich und Protektorat September 1939–September 1941* (Munich: Oldenbourg, 2012), 348.

17. Since April 1933, long before war broke out, the Nazi regime had prepared Germans for a future bombing war over Germany when it established the Reich Air Raid Protection League (Reichluftschutzbund), which obligated German civilians to train and prepare for enemy air raids. In cities, residents of an apartment building formed an independent "air-raid protection community" led by an air-raid warden (*Luftschutzwart*), a duty assigned to Gustav Becker. The air-raid warden enforced regulations, secured the building, and led the in-house fire brigade. The extinction of fires was a key mission of the often ill-equipped air-raid protection community and became increasingly dangerous as time went on and Allied bombing raids increased in frequency and severity. See Demps, "Berlin im Bombenkrieg," 358.

18. In 1940, seven religious women of the Sisters of Mercy of St. Charles Borromeo (Borromäerinnen) provided cooking and housekeeping at St. Peter Seminary in Berlin-Grünau. The Berlin seminarians primarily attended seminary at the University of Breslau, though after 1933 they were also sent to institutions of higher learning in Fulda, Frankfurt am Main, and Innsbruck. In 1932, the Berlin diocese opened its own seminary in Berlin-Grünau. This seminary offered pastoral courses to seminarians for one year following their academic training. On June 17, 1941, on order of the Gestapo, the seminary was closed and the building confiscated. It was soon turned into a hospital for wounded soldiers. See *Amtlicher Führer durch das Bistum Berlin*, 22nd ed. (Berlin: Germania, 1938), 224; Matthias Brühe, ed., *Priester Werden in Berlin: Eine kleine Festschrift anlässlich des 25jährigen Bestehens des Priesterseminars in Berlin-Zehlendorf* (Berlin: Enka, 1992); and *Schematismus des Bistums Berlin für das Jahr 1941*, 90.

19. Maria Herberg, born Mühlenbein (1889–1980), was a widow who lived in Berlin Grünau at the time. The friendship the author forged with Maria Herberg outlasted the war, and in 1964, Silvan Becker married Maria Herberg's daughter, Vera.

20. See the introduction for more information on the various camps in which Max was interned.

21. Emil Kofmehl-Steiger was a fine jeweler in Zurich, Switzerland.

22. Our Lady's Capuchin Friary (Liebfrauen), Frankfurt am Main. Founded in 1525, in central Italy, the Friars Minor Capuchins (O.F.M.Cap.) is one of three branches of Franciscan friars.

23. "Loreto Sisters," or the "English Ladies" (*Englischen Fräulein*), were informal names for the women religious congregation Institute of the Blessed Virgin Mary established by the British woman Mary Ward (1585–1645) in 1609. The sisters opened a boarding school for girls in Bensheim in 1856. In 1938, the Nazi regime closed the school along with numerous other private Catholic schools throughout Germany. Since 2004, the congregation has been known as Congregatio Jesu. "Congregatio Jesu," http://www.congregatiojesu.org/index.asp.

24. Silvan's description refers to the liturgical custom of the Holy Sepulcher (Heiliges Grab)—the burial vault of Christ—dating back to pre-Reformation times. Following the Holy Thursday Eucharist, the figure of Christ was temporarily removed from the sanctuary Crucifix or the entire Crucifix was temporarily removed from the sanctuary. In another part of the church or in the area near a side altar, a replica of the Holy Sepulcher was created in which a replica of the body of Christ was laid and adorned by Catholics. In select Catholic churches in Europe, a permanent altar dedicated to the Holy Sepulcher was erected in which permanently laid an art rendering of the body of Christ.

25. A noted institution of higher learning that continues today, the Technical University of Berlin (Technische Universität Berlin) was originally founded in 1879 as the Royal Technical Academy (Königliche Technische Hochschule) when two preexisting royal academic institutes, the Royal Mining Academy of Berlin (Königliche Bergakademie zu Berlin) and the Royal Trade Academy (Gewerbe-akademie zu Berlin), consolidated. In 1916, a third institution, the Royal Building Academy of Berlin (Königliche Bauakademie zu Berlin), also merged into the Royal Technical Academy. Following the end of imperial rule in 1918, the academy's name was changed to the Technical College of Berlin (Technische Hochschule Berlin). Like the majority of German institutions of higher learning, under National Socialism, Jewish professors and staff were subject to severe harassment and eventual termination of employment. "University History," Technical University of Berlin, http://www.tu-berlin.de/menue/ueber_die_tu_berlin/profil_geschichte/geschichte/parameter/en/.

26. The first decree for the Implementation of the Law regarding Changes of Family Names of January 5, 1938, ordered that "Jews may be given only such given names as are listed in the Guidelines on the Use of Given Names issued by the Reich Minister of the Interior." The second decree of the same law issued on August 17, 1938, stated that "insofar as Jews have other given names than those which may be given to Jews according to [the first decree], they are obligated beginning January 1, 1939, to assume an additional given name, namely, the given name Israel in the case of males, and the given name Sarah in the case of females." See Lucy S. Dawidowicz, ed., *A Holocaust Reader* (New York: Behrman House, 1976), 52–53.

27. Father Franz Telzer (1874–1952) was a priest of the Innsbruck diocese.

28. Paul Rusch (1903–1986) was ordained a bishop on November 30, 1938. Following the territorial changes after the First World War, in 1919 the regions of Innsbruck-Feldkirch were given their own apostolic delegate under the authority of the bishop of Brixen. In 1925, Innsbruck-Feldkirch was separated from the diocese of Brixen and elevated to an Apostolic Administratur led by an apostolic adminis- trator. The Holy See takes such steps as it prepares a region to become a diocese. In 1938, the Holy See appointed Bishop Rusch as Innsbruck-Feldkirch's second apostolic administrator. On November 26, 1964, Rusch became bishop of Innsbruck-Feldkirch following its elevation to a diocese. In 1968, Feldkirch was made a separate diocese and Rusch remained as bishop of Innsbruck until his resignation in 1980. Rusch had considerable problems with the National Socialists whose regional administrative district leader (Gauleiter), Franz Hofer (Tirol-Vorarlberg), refused to recognize his appointment as apostolic administrator of Innsbruck-Feldkirch. On Rusch, see Josef Gelmi, "Paul Rusch," in *Die Bischöfe der deutschsprachigen Länder 1785/1803 bis 1945: Ein biographisches Lexikon*, ed. Erwin Gatz (Berlin: Duncker & Humblot, 1983), 637–638.

29. Monsignor Michael Weiskopf (1890–1966) was head of the Office of Pastoral Care (Seelsorgeamtsleiter) for the Innsbruck-Feldkirch Apostolic Administratur. Following the Second World War, he continued his administrative service to the diocese, eventually serving as its vicar general (1964–1966). On Weiskopf, see Josef Franckenstein, "Michael Weiskopf," in Gelmi, *Die Bischöfe der deutschsprachigen Länder 1785/1803 bis 1945*, 279–280.

30. Erna makes an error here in her recollection. *Das Schwarze Korps* (the Black Corps) was the official newspaper of SS, published from 1935 to 1945. On this newspaper, see William Combs, *Voice of the SS: A History of the SS Journal Das Schwarze Korps* (New York: Peter Lang, 1986). *Der Stürmer*, under the editorship of Julius Streicher and published from 1923 to 1945, was an extremely crude antisemitic tabloid. On *Der Stürmer*, see Randall L. Bytwerk, *Julius Streicher: The Man Who Persuaded a Nation to Hate Jews* (New York: Stein and Day, 1983); and Dennis E. Showalter, *Little Man What Now? Der Stürmer in the Weimer Republic* (Hamden, CT: Archon Books, 1982).

31. Dr. Margarete Merzbach (b. 1897) was married to Dr. Ludwig Hermann Merzbach (b. 1896). Their daughter, Uta, was born on February 9, 1933.

32. In the November 14, 1935, First Supplement to the Reich Citizenship Law, the German National Socialist government changed its earlier definition of who was a Jew. The case of Dr. Margarete Merzbach pointedly illustrates the complexity of the government's endeavor. In their efforts to define the "Jewish race," the Nazis relied on both marital status and religious affiliation. The First Supplement to the Reich Citizenship Law would ordinarily have defined Dr. Margarete Merzbach as a "Mischling" (person of mixed blood) of the first degree because she was half-Jewish with presumably two Jewish grandparents. In Nazi Germany, "persons of mixed blood" experienced various forms of discrimination and persecution that

nonetheless differed in degree from the persecution of Jews. However, on account of her marriage to a Jew, Dr. Merzbach lost her status as "Mischling" and was also counted as a Jew. A "person of mixed blood" who professed the Jewish faith was also counted as a Jew. By contrast, the Nazi racial laws deemed Silvan Becker, who was Roman Catholic, a "Mischling" of the first degree. On this point, see Jeremy Noakes, "The Development of Nazi Policy towards the German-Jewish 'Mischlinge' 1933–1945," in *Leo Baeck Institute Year Book* 34 (1989): 291, 313, 324–326.

33. St. Francis Xavier parish (St. Franziskus Xaverius) in Berlin-East (today Berlin-Mitte).

34. December 26 is the feast day of St. Stephen, the first Christian martyr whose story is told in chapters 6 and 7 of the Acts of the Apostles. In many European countries, including Germany, the day following Christmas is also a national holiday.

35. Erna identifies the priest only with the first initial of his last name. She refers to him in German as *Pater*, the term used for priests who were members of a religious community. Other than this information, he is unidentifiable.

36. St. Francis Xavier Home (Xaveriusstift) at Kaiserstrasse 36a (now Jacobystrasse) in Berlin-East (today Berlin-Mitte) was run by the Sisters of Saint Joseph (Josephschwestern) from Trier. Its goal was to assist employed women workers economically, socially, religiously, and morally. It also provided temporary and long-term housing for single women. See *Schematismus des Bistums Berlin für das Jahr 1941*, 93.

37. Alfred Döblin's classic 1929 novel *Berlin Alexanderplatz* graphically depicted the criminality surrounding Berlin's Alexanderplatz in its telling of the fictitious story of ex-convict Franz Biberkopf's attempts at redemption in Weimar Germany. The novel became etched in German culture and influenced how Germans viewed the city streets near Alexanderplatz, located in the center of Berlin (today Berlin-Mitte). In 1980, legendary German director Rainer Werner Fassbinder directed a fifteen-hour film that enabled many Germans to discover Döblin's work anew.

38. According to a decree from September 23, 1939, Jews, including Jews in privileged marriages, had to relinquish their radios to the local police. See Blau, *Das Ausnahmerecht für die Juden*, 75, 113.

39. Dated September 1, 1939, the Decree for the Defense of the Reich on Extraordinary Radio Measures prohibited Germans from listening to foreign radio broadcasts, an act that state authorities viewed as defeatist and therefore harmful to the war effort. Punishments consisted of penal servitude or a prison sentence. Those convicted of dissemination of the content of foreign radio broadcasts faced imprisonment or death. See Ingo von Münch, ed., *Gesetze des NS-Staates: Dokumente eines Unrechtssystems*, 3rd rev. ed. (Paderborn: Ferdinand Schöningh, 1994), 229–230.

40. On September 19, 1941, the Police Order on the Marking of Jews of September 1, 1941, took effect in Germany. It ordered most Jewish Germans above the age of six years to wear a yellow star inscribed with the word "Jew" (*Jude*) on their outer clothing and their work clothes. Starting in April 1942, Jews also had to mark their homes with the Star of David. As Erna states, privileged Jews in mixed marriages were exempt from the decree. See Diemut Majer, *"Non-Germans" under the Third*

Reich: The Nazi Judicial and Administrative System in Germany and Occupied Eastern
Europe, with Special Regard to Occupied Poland, 1939–1945, trans. Peter Thomas Hill
et al., 2nd ed. (Lubbock: Texas Tech University Press, 2013), 170.

41. After marking Jews, the regime also increasingly restricted their freedom of
movement. Prohibited from driving a car since 1938, Jews depended on public
transport. But the aforementioned decree of September 1941 also confined Jewish
Germans "to their local community, which they were permitted only to leave with
the permission of the local police. The use of public transportation (except local)
was in principle prohibited, except by special police permit, and such permits were
to be 'limited to the strictest minimum.'" Between October 1941 and March 1942,
the Reich Minister of the Interior, Wilhelm Frick, further restricted Jewish Germans' use of public transportation. Now, most Jews were also prohibited from using
public transportation in their place of residence. According to historian Dietmut
Majer, "The timing of these restrictions was not accidental but was chosen to
coincide exactly with the start of large-scale deportations to the East in the fall of
1941." See Majer, *"Non-Germans" under the Third Reich,* 171–172.

42. St. Paul's parish, Oldenburger Strasse 46, in the Moabit neighborhood in
central Berlin (Berlin-Mitte).

43. On November 24, 1941, the Security Service, or Sicherheitsdienst (SD) of the
SS, reported about instructions that Cardinal Adolf Bertram, the archbishop of
Breslau and head of the German Bishops' Conference (Fulda Conference) had
issued on September 17, 1941. Bertram wrote,

The ramifications of the police ordinance concerning the conduct of Catholics in
response to Catholics of Jewish descent present at mass are bound to differ from
place to place, specifically contingent on the greater or lesser influence of attitudes
that are widespread in the general populace.

1. It is therefore imperative that hastily formulated policies that may be
seen as offensive to Jewish Catholics be avoided, such as introducing special
pews for Jews only, segregation in the dispensation of Holy Communion, the
introduction of segregated mass services for Jews only.

2. The officially sanctioned segregation and special handling of non-
Aryans violates the notion of Christian brotherly love. It is therefore to be
avoided for as long as possible. Pastors are to recommend that these Catholics seek to attend the early mass if at all possible.

3. Reminders concerning brotherly love and avoiding every form of
denigrating treatment of any Catholic non-Aryan marked by the star are to
be issued [to members of the congregation attending mass] only when and if
disturbances arise.

4. Only if and when more substantial difficulties arise (if civil servants,
party members, and others begin staying home or ostentatiously leaving
mass in protest) should the step be taken of suggesting to Catholic non-
Aryans that special Jewish-only masses be held.

5. If a reminder should prove necessary, the following text may be used:

In light of the difficulties that have arisen for Jews living in Germany as a result of the police ordinance of 1 September 1941, all Catholics are hereby reminded to demonstrate toward Christians of Jewish descent the same degree of consideration due every Christian according to the principles outlined by St. Paul: no one who believes in Christ shall be put to shame. For there is no difference between the Jews and the Greek; for the same Lord over all is rich unto all who call upon him.

For all of you who have been baptized into Christ have assumed the mantle of Christ. There is neither Jew nor Greek, there is neither bond nor free, for you are all one in Jesus Christ.

Anson Rabinbach and Sander L. Gilman, eds., *The Third Reich Sourcebook* (Berkeley: University of California Press, 2013), 427–429.

44. Father Josef Feichtner (1889–1965) was a priest of the Archdiocese of Salzburg.

45. Father Meinrad Bliem (1901–1960) was parochial vicar in Reith bei Brixlegg from 1935 to 1942.

46. Starting in the nineteenth century, travelers in Germany had to register with the local police, which was an effort to track and avert "threats" to the community. By the beginning of the twentieth century, German states, most notably Prussia and Bavaria, had extended this obligation to register their place of residence to all citizens. Compulsory registration allowed the modern nation-state to increase its oversight over its citizens, enabling it, for example, to enforce compulsory schooling and universal conscription. In January 1938, with the Decree on the System for Registration, the Nazi regime introduced a uniform system of registration for all of Germany. The new forms required registrants, in addition to their names and addresses, to disclose their religion, citizenship, military service, and membership in the air-raid protection league. As Erna points out here, landlords were also required to report the names of their tenants to the police. Most European states, including Germany, continue to maintain centralized registers of their citizens to this day. Verordnung über das Meldewesen (Reichsmeldeordnung) vom 6. Januar 1938, *Reichsgesetzblatt,* 1938, Part I, 13–28; and "Historische Geschichte des Meldewesens," Bundesministerium des Inneren, http://www.bmi.bund.de/DE/Themen/Moderne-Verwaltung/Verwaltungsrecht/Meldewesen/ Historische-Entwicklung/historische-entwicklung_node.html.

47. On May 3, 1933, Hitler established the NSV (Nationalsozialistische Volkswohlfahrt) and designated it responsible "for all matters concerning National Socialist welfare work and social services." Divided into six divisions ("organization, financial administration, welfare work and youth care, public health, propaganda, and training"), it endeavored to assist Aryan Germans in need. Inherent in its programs was promotion of the National Socialist racial ideology. See "National Socialist Volk Welfare," in *The Encyclopedia of the Third Reich,* ed.

Christian Zentner and Friedemann Bedürftig, trans. Amy Hackett (New York: Da Capo, 1997), 636–637.

48. On September 18, 1942, the Reich Minister for Food and Agriculture decreed special shopping hours for Jews. However, long before then, in July 1940, the president of police of Berlin had already restricted the shopping hours for Jews to between 4:00 p.m. and 5:00 p.m. Even though the decree exempted Jews in privileged marriages, it appears that shopkeepers ignored the directive and refused to serve Erna. Other sources corroborate this kind of localized radicalization, where ordinary Germans went beyond what official directives required of them to persecute Jews, including Jews in privileged marriages and their spouses. For instance, beginning in 1940, some shopkeepers in Berlin posted signs in their shop windows that informed Aryan spouses of Jews that, like Jews, they would only be served during certain designated hours. See Blau, *Das Ausnahmerecht für die Juden*, 117; Büttner, *Die Not der Juden teilen*, 47; and Majer, *"Non-Germans" under the Third Reich*, 677.

49. In June 1941, the NSV in Berlin announced that Jews would receive their ration cards separately from Aryan Germans. See Blau, *Das Ausnahmerecht für die Juden*, 83.

50. With the outbreak of the Second World War on September 1, 1939, the German government introduced rationing, and henceforth fat, meat, butter, milk, cheese, sugar, and jam could only be purchased with government-issued ration coupons. Later that month, bread and eggs were added to the list, and in October 1939, the state issued "clothing cards," which rationed textiles for civilians. Despite these restrictions, non-Jewish Germans suffered little hunger during the war because the regime ruthlessly plundered the occupied territories to supply the German population with food. While the German government prioritized the feeding of Aryan Germans throughout the conflict, starting in 1939, Jewish Germans received fewer rations, and these were rigorously cut over the following years. As Erna writes, by the summer of 1942, Jews' rations no longer included sugar or white bread. Beginning in 1941, the situation of Jews became increasingly precarious, as most could also no longer obtain meat, butter, fruit, vegetables, or coffee. Furthermore, it was extremely difficult for Jews to supplement their rations because the state forbade Jews to purchase nonrationed foodstuffs, such as fish, and deducted from their rations the contents of the food parcels that some Jews received from relatives overseas. However, the extent to which Erna was still affected by these restrictions in 1942 is unclear because in early 1940, the regime exempted Jews in privileged marriages from ration cuts imposed on all other Jews as well as from the requirement to mark their ration cards with a "J." Subsequent decrees from July 1941 and July 1942 reiterated these exemptions for privileged Jews, but Ursula Büttner also found that some local authorities ignored these directives. See Blau, *Das Ausnahmerecht für die Juden*, 118; Büttner, *Die Not der Juden teilen*, 48; Lizzie Collingham, *The Taste of War: World War II and the Battle for Food* (New York: Penguin, 2011), 155–164, 359; and Walk, *Das Sonderrecht für die Juden*, 314, 318–319, 339.

51. Erna refers here to a nurse belonging to the Nursing Association of the National Socialist Welfare Association (Schwesternschaft der Nationalsozialistischen Volkswohlfahrt).

52. As they did to most Jewish Germans, the authorities evicted the Merzbach family from their home and forced them to move into a designated "Jew house" (*Judenhaus*), where they lived in overcrowded and dismal conditions. This was no accident, as is shown, for example, in September 1941, when the Gestapo Düsseldorf admonished local authorities that "The Jews are to be assigned only the dirtiest and worst accommodation, whilst current sanitary regulations must be observed." Since "Jew houses" had to be accessible to authorities at all times, Jewish tenants were subject to random "inspections," acts of violence, and looting by Gestapo officials and others. See Marlis Buchholz and Konard Kwiet, "Judenhäuser in Germany," in *The Yad Vashem Encyclopedia of the Ghettos during the Holocaust*, vol. 2, ed. Guy Miron and Shlomit Shulani (Jerusalem: Yad Vashem, 2009), 999–1001.

53. Erna's statement must be read with caution. Dr. Ludwig Merzbach most certainly did not direct deportations of Jews to the east. However, a Gestapo transport list to Terezin from July 1, 1943, includes the notation that Dr. Ludwig Merzbach had worked for the Reich Association of Jews in Germany (Reichsvereinigung der Juden in Deutschland) and that he had assisted with the transports of Jews. This notation touches on one of the most sinister aspects of the Holocaust, namely, the Nazis' forced involvement of Jews in the deportations. Starting in the fall of 1941, the Reich Main Security Office (Reichssicherheitshauptamt, or RSHA) under Reinhard Heydrich (1904–1942) and the Gestapo compelled the Reich Association of Jews in Germany, where Dr. Ludwig Merzbach worked, to assist them in carrying out the deportations of Jewish Germans. Established in July 1939 by decree, initially, the Reich Association's main tasks were the dissemination of orders and information as well as the organization and coordination of mass emigration, social welfare, and the Jewish school system. According to the historian Beate Meyers, its Jewish leaders viewed the organization "as a mouthpiece to represent the interest of the Jews vis-à-vis the Nazi German state." Dr. Ludwig Merzbach worked as an auditor in the Reich Association's main office in Berlin. His department oversaw the finances and accounting practices of the organization's regional offices. It is unclear how his role of auditor intersected with the deportation of Jews to the East, but the Reich Association and its district branches did send large quantities of furnishings to Theresienstadt in 1942, a matter that probably involved Dr. Merzbach's department. See Gestapo Transport list of the 94th Alterstransport, 1.2.1.1/11194066 /ITS, http://1.2.1.1/11194066/ITS, Digital Archive, USHMM; and Beate Meyer, *A Fateful Balancing Act: The Dilemma of the Reich Association of Jews in Germany, 1939–1945* (New York: Berghahn Books, 2011), 3, 29, 160, 226.

54. Julius Streicher, the editor of *Der Stürmer*, worked with local Nazi Party officials to publicly mount boards or cases to display the newspaper in towns throughout Germany to ensure a wide readership. See Showalter, *Little Man What Now?*, 74.

55. On the night of March 1–2, 1943, the allies bombed Berlin and directly hit St. Hedwig's Catholic Cathedral in central Berlin. A raging fire burned for two hours and almost nothing remained. Joseph Goebbels, the Reich Minister for Propaganda and Enlightenment, recorded in his diary entry of March 3, 1943: "Berlin had gone through a bad air raid during the night. . . . A tremendous number of places have been damaged. Industrial plants and public buildings have been badly hit. St. Hedwig's Cathedral was burned to the ground, and besides four other churches and a number of hospitals, homes for the aged, et cetera." Josef Goebbels, *The Goebbels Diaries 1942–1943*, ed. and trans. Louis P. Lochner (New York: Doubleday, 1948), 269.

56. The Blessed Sacrament is the bread and wine consecrated during the Mass to become the body and blood of Christ. The blood of Christ is regularly consumed in its entirety during the Mass. The body of Christ is also consumed; however, whatever hosts are not consumed are reserved in a church's tabernacle for reverence and for Communion for the sick and infirm who are unable to attend Mass.

57. Erna was arrested during the so-called Factory Action (*Fabrikaktion*), a nationwide campaign against Jews that was coordinated by the RSHA under the leadership of SS Obergruppenführer Ernst Kaltenbrunner (1903–1946). The Factory Action began on February 27, 1943, and marked the beginning of the final push to bring the mass deportations of German Jews to a conclusion. At the beginning of 1943, two-thirds of the approximately 51,320 Jews who remained in Germany lived in Berlin, and for this reason, Berlin was the main focus of the Factory Action. Many of the remaining Jews were forced laborers who had previously been exempt from deportation because they worked in armament factories. In February 1943, many Jews were indeed seized at their places of work, but the Gestapo did not limit their arrests to Jewish forced laborers in factories, but also arrested Jews on the street and in their apartments. Because of the large numbers of Jews living in Berlin in 1943, soldiers of the Waffen-SS assisted the Gestapo in the arrests of Jews that dragged on for an entire week. This explains why Erna was targeted so late in the campaign. See Gruner, *Widerstand in der Rosenstrasse*, 46–61.

58. From 1671, the Grosse Hamburger Strasse was the site of a Jewish cemetery, and in the nineteenth century, the Jewish community opened a school and rest home for seniors adjacent to it. In March 1942, the RSHA closed the rest home and school and converted the buildings into a transit camp for Jews. During the Factory Action, the camp Grosse Hamburger Strasse was one of several sites in Berlin where the Gestapo detained Jews. Toward the end of the Factory Action, after the RSHA had already started to deport Jews from other transit camps to Auschwitz, all newly detained Jews like Erna were taken to the camp Grosse Hamburger Strasse. See Gruner, *Widerstand in der Rosenstrasse*, 70; and Ulrich Eckhardt and Andreas Nachama, *Jüdische Orte in Berlin* (Berlin: Nicolaische, 2005), 20–22.

59. In describing her almost immediate release from the camp Grosse Hamburger Strasse, Erna touched on the most controversial issues surrounding the Factory Action, namely, whether or not the Nazis intended to deport Jews living in

privileged marriages to Auschwitz along with nonprivileged Jews arrested during the campaign. Erna's fellow detainees in the Grosse Hamburger Strasse were justified in their fears of immediate deportation to the Łódź Ghetto, then known as Litzmannstadt in Germany, because within days of the commencement of the Factory Action, on March 1, 1943, the RSHA started to deport Jews to Auschwitz. Wolf Gruner writes that in the course of the campaign, the regime deported approximately 11,000 Jews to Auschwitz but almost no privileged Jews were among them because the regime never intended to deport them in the first place. Gruner argues that the Gestapo arrested privileged Jews for the purpose of reorganizing their forced-labor assignments, and for this reason, many privileged Jews who were arrested during the Factory Action were let go almost immediately, especially if they were taken late in the campaign as Erna was. Thus, Erna's experience appears to support Gruner's conclusions but other scholars, most notably Nathan Stoltzfus, argue that the Nazis had indeed intended to deport privileged Jews during the Factory Action and that it was only after the courageous protest of their Ayran spouses outside of the camp in the Rosenstrasse that the regime relented and decided to release the privileged Jews held in that camp. See Gruner, *Widerstand in der Rosenstrasse*, 71–76, 97–136; and Nathan Stoltzfus, *Resistance of the Heart: Intermarriage and the Rosenstrasse Protest in Nazi Germany* (New York: Norton, 1996).

60. St. Hedwig Hospital (St. Hedwig Krankenhaus), Grosse Hamburger Strasse 5–11 in Berlin-West (today Berlin-Mitte).

61. The Sisters of Mercy of St. Charles Borromeo (Borromäerinnen) from Trier served at St. Hedwig Hospital.

62. Father Georg von Unold (1895–1969) was the Berlin diocesan priest assigned to St. Hedwig Hospital as chaplain. He began his ministry there in February 1940.

63. According to eyewitnesses, during the Factory Action, the Gestapo indeed arrested Jews at ration card distribution offices. However, the extant literature on the Factory Action makes no mention of the fact that the regime rearrested Jews who had been released. It is possible that Erna was inadvertently describing new arrests of Jews who had escaped the Gestapo's dragnet until that point. See Gruner, *Widerstand in der Rosenstrasse*, 65.

64. According to Dr. Uta Merzbach, the daughter of Drs. Margarete and Ludwig Merzbach, the family was indeed arrested and held in the transit camp Grosse Hamburger Strasse in Berlin, from where they were deported to the concentration camp Theresienstadt on August 4, 1943. Uta Merzbach, email message to editors, November 1, 2015; and Gestapo transport list transcribed on April 4, 1944: 95th Alterstransport deported on August 4, 1943, 1.2.1.1.,11194093, ITS Digital Archive, USHMM.

65. As outlined above, starting in the spring of 1940, the German labor office compelled all Jews deemed fit for work, including Jews in mixed marriages, to perform forced labor. When Erna received her summons to the labor office in April 1943, forced labor policies were once again in flux, as the vast majority of the

remaining 15,000 Jewish German laborers in Berlin had been deported east and were subsequently murdered in the course of the Factory Action. The remaining privileged Jews were now forced to perform heavy, manual labor rather than work in industry as before. See especially Gruner, *Jewish Forced Labor*, 32–82.

66. See the introduction for background information on Erna's brother Max.

67. Religious medals have their roots in pre-Christian amulets that were worn for protection to ward off evil. Since the earliest days of Christianity, followers of Christ have created, worn, and carried medals stamped with the image of saints or images relating to saints or religious events. Religious medals are worn for devotional purposes to draw an individual closer to Christ through the intercession of a particular saint. Here Erna refers to a medal bearing the image of St. Benedict. The St. Benedict medal is one of the more popular Catholic medals whose history is recounted in the classic work by Prosper Guéranger, *The Medal or Cross of St. Benedict: Its Origins, Meaning, and Privileges*, originally published in 1880 and consistently reprinted over the years.

68. Located near Oberammergau in Bavaria and founded in 1330, the Benedictine abbey Ettal became an important religious center by the eighteenth century and it continues to attract countless visitors to this day, in part on account of its impressive Baroque church. The town of Erkner is located on the southeastern edge of Berlin.

69. Father Lukas Menz, O.S.B. (1898–1961). Ordained on July 26, 1932, by Cardinal Michael von Faulhaber, archbishop of Munich and Freising, Father Menz initially taught modern languages at the Ettal Gymnasium until 1938 when the preparatory school was closed. After the closure, he served in a variety of internal ministries of the Ettal abbey including its publishing house. With the shortage of parish priests during the war years, from 1943 to 1945, Father Menz became parochial vicar at the Catholic parish in Bruckberg bei Landshut, Bavaria, northeast of Munich. Following the war, after the Gymnasium reopened, Father Menz returned to teaching. On Menz, see Death Notice, Ettal, December 12, 1961, Archiv der Benediktinerarbtei Ettal.

70. Although no specific order for evacuation may be found on this date, on June 14, 1943, Joseph Goebbels wrote in an urgent directive (*Schnellbrief*), "The evacuation of the section of the population that is not engaged in war production efforts in cities severely damaged by aerial warfare is a pressing imperative. Nevertheless, we will refrain from a forced evacuation for psychological reasons." Afterward, Goebbels did consult with Hitler and further directives for evacuation were issued. Over the summer of 1943, more than 680,000 people fled Berlin for the safety of the countryside. The deadly allied aerial bombing of Hamburg in late July 1943 intensified this flight pattern. See Laurenz Demps, ed., *Luftangriffe auf Berlin: Die Berichte der Hauptluftschutzstelle 1940–1945* (Berlin: Christoph Links, 2012), 72–81, here 73.

71. Binosa Zobl, born Weirather (1874–1944).

72. Siegfried Matthäus Zobl (1909–1994).

73. During the war, the German government forced the churches to hand over church bells to the state because metals were in short supply and they were needed in the production of war materials. See Dietrich Eichholtz, *Geschichte der deutschen Kriegswirtschaft*, vol. 1, *1939–1941* (Munich: K. G. Saur, 2003), 369.

74. Josef Peter was mayor of Tannheim from April 1, 1939 to January 4, 1945.

75. A postal identity card (*Postausweis*) was an internationally recognized identification card issued by "post offices in the member states of the Universal Postal Union under the terms of the world postal treaties of 1920 and 1925." See Jane Caplan, "'Ausweis Bitte!' Identity and Identification in Nazi Germany," in *Identification and Registration Practices in Transnational Perspective: People, Papers and Practices*, ed. Ilsen About, James Brown, and Gayle Lonergan (New York: Palgrave Macmillan, 2013), 233.

76. Aryan physicians were permitted to treat Jews only in case of an emergency, when a Jewish physician was unavailable. There were, of course, few Jewish physicians left in Germany at the time of Erna's accident in 1943. In July 1938 the Nazi regime had rescinded Jewish physicians' medical licenses, and scholars estimate that about 75 percent of the approximately 6,000 Jewish German physicians living in Nazi Germany emigrated. They were joined by about 2,500 Jewish Austrian physicians. Although the German state permitted some of the remaining Jewish physicians to continue to treat Jewish patients as "Krankenbehandler," a deliberately demeaning and clumsy title that literally translates as "caregiver for the sick," their numbers were small and they practiced mostly in cities. Jews in rural areas lost virtually all access to medical care. Hospitals, too, became increasingly unwilling to treat Jewish patients. In 1936, the mayor of Düsseldorf decreed that municipal hospitals would no longer admit Jewish patients. Thereafter, Jews were treated only on an outpatient basis. In 1938, the Ministry of the Interior ordered hospitals that still admitted Jews to segregate them from Aryan patients in order to avoid the possibility of "race defilement." See Rebecca Schwoch, "'Praktisch zum Verhungern verurteilt': 'Krankenbehandler' zwischen 1938 und 1945," in *Jüdische Ärztinnen und Ärzte im Nationalsozialismus: Entrechtung, Vertreibung, Ermordung*, ed. Thomas Beddies, Susanne Doetz, and Christoph Kopke (Berlin: de Gruyter, 2014), 78; Anna E. von Villiez, "Emigration jüdischer Ärzte im Nationalsozialismus," in Beddies, Doetz, and Kopke, *Jüdische Ärztinnen und Ärzte im Nationalsozialismus*, 191; and Walk, *Das Sonderrecht für die Juden*, 166, 230.

77. The farmer's name was Michl Lochbihler.

78. "Grüss Gott," is a common greeting used in Southern Germany and Austria. Popularized in the nineteenth century by the Catholic clergy, it is short for "May God Bless You" (*Grüsse Dich Gott*). In this context, the German verb "grüssen" does not mean "to greet" but "to bless."

79. University professor Virgil Redlich, O.S.B. (1890–1970).

80. Located in the historic section in the city of Salzburg, Nonnberg Abbey is the oldest women's cloister north of the Alps that can boast of an uninterrupted existence since its founding in the early eighth century. "Abtei Nonnberg," http://www

.benediktinerinnen.de/index.php/adressen/2-uncategorised/26-nonnberg.
University professor Alois Mager, O.S.B. (1881–1946).

81. Introduced during the Reformation by Martin Luther, the Christ Child
(*Christkind*) as gift giver counteracted the Catholic emphasis on St. Nicholas.
Historian Joe Perry explains,

> By the late nineteenth century, in popular observance, Luther's ascetic Holy
> Christ had metamorphosed into the sentimental *Christkind*. This androgynous
> being appeared in contemporary illustrations as an angel in the form of a young boy
> or girl sporting wings, a flowing white gown, and a halo. The *Christkind* usually
> brought children gifts, a candle, and/or a Christmas tree.... The *Christkind*, despite
> his Lutheran roots, was especially popular in Catholic households because of his
> lingering associations with Jesus.

See Joe Perry, *Christmas in Germany: A Cultural History* (Chapel Hill: University
of North Carolina Press, 2010), 36.

82. From 1937 to 1945, Dr. Ferdinand Waller (1879–1949) was the county commissioner (*Landrat*) of the district of Sonthofen.

83. The proprietor's name was actually Johann Konrad Fink (1874–1951). The
Alpengasthof "Zur Post" in Schattwald remains open to this day.

84. Lourdes Chapel (Lourdeskapelle) is located in the countryside in the village
of Zöblin.

85. Prejudices against Sinti and Roma ("gypsies") in fact were widespread in
modern Germany. The Nazis persecuted Sinti and Roma throughout occupied
Europe, murdering between 250,000 and 500,000 of them in the Holocaust. See
Sybil H. Milton, "'Gypsies' as Social Outsiders in Nazi Germany," in *Social
Outsiders in Nazi Germany*, ed. Robert Gellately and Nathan Stoltzfus (Princeton,
NJ: Princeton University Press, 2001), 212.

86. Digitalis is a drug derived from the dried leaves of the common foxglove and
used in heart medicine. It was discovered and first prescribed by the English physician
William Withering (1741–1799) in the eighteenth century. Administered correctly,
digitalis reduces fluid retention and eases breathlessness in individuals with conges-
tive heart failure, but in high doses it can be fatal. See Thomas Dormandy, *The White
Death: A History of Tuberculosis* (London: Hambledon, 2001), 17.

87. Most likely, Erna stayed with Maria Josefa Dinser, born Weber (1898–1983).

88. St. John the Baptist (St. Johannes der Täufer). Father Max Pfau (1888–1975)
was the pastor. Twice under National Socialism, Pfau had problems with the state
authorities. In 1933, the local police questioned him for spreading writings considered hostile to the state. In 1936, while pastor in Hindelang, he received a warning
from the police to disband his newly founded parish chapter of the St. Michael's
Association designed to foster Catholic literature. See Monatsberichte der Regier-
ung, Augsburg, December 6, 1936, in Helmut Witetschek, ed., *Die Kirchliche Lage in
Bayern 1933–1943 III: Regierungsbezirk Schwaben* (Mainz: Matthias-Grünewald,
1971), 115; and Ulrich von Hehl et al., eds., *Priester unter Hitlers Terror: Eine*

Biographische und Statistische Erhebung, 4th ed. (Paderborn: Ferdinand Schöningh, 1998), 394.

89. A directive issued by Hitler's chancellery on June 26, 1941, excluded "persons of mixed blood" of the first degree from all German schools, except for the basic Volksschule. The Volksschule comprised four years of elementary school and an additional four years of schooling. According to this directive, the village teacher should have enrolled Silvan in his school. He thus went beyond what was required of him by law to persecute Jews. See H. G. Adler, *Der Verwaltete Mensch: Studien zur Deportation der Juden aus Deutschland* (Tübingen: Mohr, 1974), 296.

90. Father Josef Huber (1886–1967) was pastor of St. Andrew parish (St. Andreas). Huber had an extensive record of conflicts with state authorities, primarily arising from his pastoral ministry. In 1936, local National Socialist leaders interrogated him about his preaching, which was viewed as hostile to the state. In 1937, the local police questioned and warned him against taking up unauthorized collections in the church. In 1940, he was questioned and warned against his pastoral outreach to parish youth. A year later, he was questioned and fined 30 reichmarks for publishing a book without the required membership in the Reich Writer's Chamber (Reichs-schrifttumskamer). On September 30, 1941, Huber's repeated "hostile" actions toward the state led to his being prohibited from teaching. In Germany, parish priests often teach religious education in local schools, both private and public, a practice that continues today. Finally, in 1944, the local police interrogated him for illegally teaching religious education to children in a country camp (Kinderlandverschickungslager), designed during the war to offer children safe housing far away from areas subject to aerial bombing. On Huber, see Hehl et al., *Priester unter Hitlers Terror,* 363.

91. Martin Haff was mayor of Pfronten from 1935 to 1945.

92. The hospital St. Vinzenz Klinik in Pfronten was operated by the Catholic congregation of the Daughters of Charity of St. Vincent de Paul, whose sisters had been caring for orphans and the sick in Pfronten since 1898.

93. Sister M. Cherubina Koppelhuber (1895–1975) was the mother superior of the community of the Daughters of Charity of St. Vincent de Paul in Pfronten from June 1938 to October 1969. Having grown up in a large, Catholic, middle-class family in Weilheim (Germany), she entered the congregation at the age of twenty-one and trained as a nurse and laboratory technician. She was known for her kindness and tact in her dealings with others. Schwester M. Cherubina Koppelhuber, Nekrolog, Kongregationsarchiv der Barmherzigen Schwestern vom Heiligen Vinzenz von Paul, Mutterhaus Augsburg (BSAugA).

94. Sister M. Ingeborg Schmautz (1903–1979) was born in Ingolstadt (Germany). She was herself an orphan. In childhood, she and her five siblings lost their parents, and she grew up in the School Sisters of Notre Dame's orphanage in Ingolstadt. The School Sisters also trained her as a kindergarten teacher but rather than enter that congregation, at the age of twenty-four, she joined the community of the Daughters of Charity of St. Vincent de Paul. She served in the orphanage in Pfronten from 1930 to 1958. Although there are no records of Silvan and Erna Becker's stay in the

orphanage, some sisters recalled that Sister Ingeborg gave up her bed for guests staying at the orphanage on several occasions. Schwester M. Ingeborg Schmautz, Nekrolog, BSAugA.

95. In a final attempt to compel Aryan Germans to divorce their Jewish partners, and amid severe labor shortages in the final year of the war, the regime decreed on October 14, 1944, that all able-bodied men married to Jews would be conscripted into forced labor battalions of the civil engineering group Organization Todt (OT). Founded in 1938, Organization Todt was named after and initially headed by Fritz Todt (1891–1942), who was later appointed inspector general of road construction and minister of armaments. The organization was responsible for carrying out large-scale building and construction projects in support of the war effort such as the construction of the Atlantic Wall. Hitler's chief architect, Albert Speer (1905–1981), succeeded Todt after the latter's death in a plane crash in 1942. Whereas in the beginning, the OT employed mostly paid volunteers, starting in 1943, the organization increasingly relied on foreign forced laborers and prisoners of war, who, like Gustav Becker, had to labor under the most difficult conditions on OT construction sites. By the end of 1944, the Organization Todt commanded well over 1 million workers. See "Die 'Organisation Todt,'" https://www.dhm.de/lemo/kapitel/ns-regime/ns-organisationen/organisation-todt.html; and Dieter Maier, *Arbeitseinsatz und Deportation: Die Mitwirkung der Arbeitsverwaltung bei der nationalsozialistischen Judenverfolgung in den Jahren 1938–1945* (Berlin: Hentrich, 1994), 225.

96. Until 1945, St. Anna was the friary church of the Franciscans who had been in Reutte since 1628. The administrator of the friary church was Father Amatius Bilgermeier. However, it is unclear with whom Erna spoke. Since 1945, St. Anna has served as the town's parish church.

97. Purification of the Virgin Mary Church (Mariä Reinigung). Father Alois Plunser (1904–1969) served as pastor of this parish in Bach in Lechtal, Austria (at that time a part of the German Reich).

98. From April 16, 1943 to May 8, 1945, Dr. Heinrich Praxmarer served as the district commissioner of Reutte.

99. Father Thomas Innerhofer (1905–1983) was the pastor of Saint Martin parish in Häselgehr. Father Franz Berger (1893–1956) served as parochial vicar (Kaplan) at the parish.

100. Father Johann Allgäuer (1897–1973) was pastor (Expositus) of St. Michael the Archangel (St. Michel die Erzengel) parish in Stanzach.

101. Father Gebhard Hammerle (1913–1992) was the administrator of St. Mary of the Snow parish (Mariä Schnee) in Bschlabs.

102. Father Lorenz Greiter (1901–1984) was the pastor of St. Nicholaus parish (St. Nikolaus) in Elbigenalp. He was assisted part-time (*Frühmessbenefiziat*) by Father Karl Schedler (d. 1964). It appears that Erna is describing her experiences with the pastor, Father Greiter.

103. Universitätsklinikum Halle (Saale) of the Friedrich University, Halle-Wittenberg, today the Martin Luther University of Halle-Wittenberg. See

http://www.medizin.uni-halle.de/fileadmin/Bereichsordner/Menu_kopf/Presse
/Flyer_UKH_Fak_Geschichte.pdf.

104. Gustav was likely interned in the labor camp Zöschen near Merseburg. The
camp in Zöschen was opened in 1944 after the nearby labor camp Spergau was
heavily damaged during air raids. See "AEL Spergau und Zöschen," http://www
.geschichtswerkstatt-merseburg.de/historische-und-erinnerungsorte/ael-spergau
-und-zoeschen.php.

105. In 1945, Dr. Gabriel Prenner was the chief physician (*Primarius*) at St. Vincent Hospital in Zams. See http://www.landeck.tirol.gv.at/gemeindeamt/down
load/221748894_1.pdf.

106. See note 90 for information on Father Josef Huber. Father Huber also served
as an adviser (*Geistlicher Rat*) to Joseph Kumpfmüller (1869–1949), bishop of
Augsburg (1930–1949).

107. At that time, this would have been approximately US$200. The equivalent in
modern buying power would be approximately, $2,597. See Harold Marcuse, "His-
torical Currency," http://www.history.ucsb.edu/faculty/marcuse/projects/cur
rency.htm#infcalc.

108. Father Karl Knapp (1882–1970) was pastor of St. Andrew parish (St. Andreas)
in Zams.

109. See the June 1941 diary entry.

110. Here Erna misspelled the family's name, which was Haselwanter. Her
hostess was Roberta Haselwanter (1906–1966). Roberta was married to Albert Haselwanter, who was born in 1903, and at the end of 1944, went missing while serving as
a soldier on the Eastern Front.

111. Curiously, the author makes another error here, whether or not this was
deliberate we cannot know. According to the local historian of Pettnau, Mr. Rudolf
Döttlinger, the name of the farmer who hosted Erna in Pettnau was likely Peter
Kleinhans. He died in November 1971 at the age of eighty-four. Peter Kleinhans had
seven children. Perhaps his cantankerous nature can be explained in part by the loss
of two of his four sons. In August 1943, Paul Kleinhans died in battle at the age of
twenty-one, and in 1944, Franz Kleinhans went missing while serving on the
Eastern Front.

112. Maria Ladner (1900–1982) had three sons, Josef (b. 1932), Franz (1932–1999),
and Johann (b. 1934), and one daughter, Paula (d. 1996). Erna developed a close
friendship with the Ladners, and she and Silvan continued to visit the family until
the 1970s.

113. Most likely, the author is referring to Dr. Hans Hirnigel (1901–1990), who
was commissioner of the district of Innsbruck from April 26, 1938 to May 8, 1945.

114. Erna identifies the priest as Father Baron Bettenburg later in this diary
entry.

115. Father (Kommorant) Klemens von Bettenburg (1878–1946).

116. Here Erna uses the German word "*Landsleute,*" which literally means
"countrymen" and seems to refer to her fellow Germans. At this point in time, after

surviving years of persecution and having knowledge of the persecution and murder of Jews throughout Europe, it is striking that Erna would employ such language to refer to non-Jewish Germans.

117. The proprietor of the Oettl Inn was Josef Oettl (1903–1983). As the author writes, in May 1945, the Americans arrested him as a National Socialist, and as a prisoner he was dispatched for approximately six months to the Austrian village of Grins to assist in reconstruction work there. Josef Oettl was married to Frieda Oettl (1903–1991). The couple had six children.

118. Father Alois Köll (1891–1962) was the pastor of St. George parish (St. Georg) in Leiblfing. This was also the parish that served the Catholics from Pettnau.

119. Attempts to identify the servicemen recorded in the memoir were unsuccessful.

120. Emil Kofmehl-Steiger was a fine jeweler in Zurich, Switzerland.

121. Since 1095, a Benedictine monastery had existed in this region, although earlier forms of monasticism have also been recorded dating back to the sixth century. In 1806, during secularization, the abbey was forcibly closed. In 1854, Cistercian monks from Wettingen, Switzerland, moved to Bregenz in the Vorarlberg region and purchased the former abbey in order to found Wettingen-Mehrerau Abbey. Cistercian monks continue to reside in the abbey today. See "Geschichte," Zisterzienerabtei Wettingen-Mehrerau, http://www.mehrerau.at/de/abendlaendisches-moenchtum.

122. Father Friedrich Schöch (1900–1956) was pastor (Rektor) of Sacred Heart Church (Herz-Jesu-Kirche) in Bregenz from 1940 to 1946.

123. Founded in 1923 and dedicated to Our Lady Comforter of the Afflicted (Maria, Heil der Kranken), Mehrerau Sanitarium, was built on sulfur rich land and originally intended as a place of cure. The Cistercian monks of Wittingen-Mehrerau Abbey oversee its operation. Soon after its establishment, it also took on long-term rehabilitative care. On its history, see Markus Hämmerle, "Das neue Sanatorium," Sanatorium-Mehrerau, http://www.sanatorium-mehrerau.at/index.php?id=21; and "Sanatorium Mehrerau," Zisterzienerabtei Wettingen-Mehrerau, http://www.mehrerau.at/de /sanatorium-mehrerau.

124. Father Dr. Paul Anton Sinz, O.Cist. (1893–1979). In 1941, the National Socialists dissolved Mehrerau Abbey and confiscated the abbey buildings. Father Paul sought refuge at St. Blaise (Sankt Blasius), the Catholic parish in Weiler im Allgäu in the Augsburg diocese. After the war, he returned to Mehrerau to assist with the reestablishment of the abbey and resume teaching natural history at the Mehrerau Gymnasium. He also became director of the school's theater.

125. See the introduction for information on Erna's brother, Max Kohen.

126. The Merzbach family in fact survived the war and subsequently emigrated to the United States. See the introduction for further information.

127. This league could not be identified, despite numerous inquiries.

128. Gustav's weight of 50 kilograms is equivalent to 110 pounds; 1.76 meters is equivalent to 5 feet, 9 inches.

129. Extant records about forced labor camps in Berlin are incomplete, but scholars have been able to identify more than 1,000 forced labor camps in and around National Socialist Berlin. In the Grunewald district, today the district of Charlottenburg-Wilmersdorf, a labor camp was located in the Hallensee Strasse 31. It is possible that Gustav reported to that camp. See "Berlin," http://www.zwangsarbeit -forschung.de/Lagerstandorte/Berlin/berlin.html; and Rainer Kubatzki, *Zwangsar- beiter- und Kriegsgefangenenlager: Standorte und Topographie in Berlin und im branden- burgischen Umland 1939–1945. Eine Dokumentation* (Berlin: A. Spitz, 2001).

130. The Leunewerke was a chemical plant founded during the First World War in 1916 by the German chemical concern BASF. The plant initially produced ammonia for the production of explosives and chemical fertilizers. In 1925, BASF, and with it the Leunawerke, became part of the newly founded German chemical conglomerate I. G. Farbenindustrie AG (IG Farben). With the rise of National Socialism in 1933, the Leunawerke also began to focus on the production of synthetic fuels. After the outbreak of war in 1939, IG Farben expanded the Leunawerke's facilities for the production of synthetic airplane fuel and chemical fertilizers. In May 1944, the Leunawerke suffered the first of twenty-two Allied bombing attacks that left the plant heavily damaged by the spring of 1945. Slave laborers who were forced to work in the plant were liberated on April 14, 1945. See "Leuna," http://www.deutsches-chemie -museum.de/index.php?id=38.

131. Gustav Becker suffered from a tuberculous (TB) infection of the vertebral bodies, also known as Pott disease, which is an uncommon complication today, and was uncommon even in the 1940s before effective antituberculous therapy. The TB infection could and did destroy the vertebrae, which had the possibility of making the spine unstable and causing compression of the spinal cord, leading to paralysis. The total body cast prevented Becker from "flopping over" and crushing his spinal cord. In order to heal the partially destroyed vertebrae, Becker needed to have cartilage rebuild itself in the area that had been eaten away by the TB infection; hence Erna's description of the "formation of stable cartilage." The new cartilage would serve as the scaffold for new calcium deposition, forming new bone in the ruined vertebrae. This process of new cartilage formation is what is meant by "car- tilaginification." The term then is not really a diagnosis but a description of part of the healing process. Gustav was perhaps mistaken in attributing the collapse of his vertebrae to an ulceration caused by a thrombosis in his leg. Although an ulceration in his leg could have served as the portal of entry for the tuberculosis, it is more likely that the thrombosis and ulceration occurred after he had been immobi- lized and bedbound for some time. The editors would like to thank J. S. Hughes, MD, for this explanation.

132. Stella Matutina was a former Gymnasium in Feldkirch, Austria. Following the annexation of Austria to the German Reich in 1938, the school was forcibly closed. Following the war, in 1946 it reopened and remained open until its final closing in 1979. See "Die Jesuiten in Feldkirch," Jesuiten, http://www.jesuiten.at /index.php?id=142/.

133. Silvan refers to the Catholic tradition of sainthood and relics. Relics are either parts of a saint's body (first-class relic) or an item touched by a saint (second-class relic). The relic itself is not an item of worship or veneration; rather it is sacred and preserved in order to draw a person closer to the associated saint who, in turn, intercedes with God on behalf of the living individual. Thus relics help Catholics to grow closer in their relationship with the Triune God.

134. Hermann Cohen (1842–1918), a Jewish philosopher, developed the concept of what has become known as ethical monotheism. Philosopher Scott Edgar explains, "Cohen argues, since reason is a 'universal human power' that belongs to all humanity, a religion of reason cannot recognize different gods for different people, but must recognize a single, unique God for all humanity. Since the idea of such a God first emerged in history with Judaism, it is the original source of a religion of reason. Consequently, the investigation of a religion of reason must recover that religion's source by interpreting the historical scriptures and liturgical practices of Judaism. According to Cohen, monotheism, and so too Judaism, was the historical source of the idea that all humanity could be unified by a single set of ethical laws. As Cohen sees it, God is the set of ideal ethical laws. To assert that there is only one God for all of humanity is thus to assert a universal ethical ideal, one on which individuals see all people as 'fellow humans,' and not as 'others' who can be excluded from the moral community." Whether Erna was well-versed in Cohen's thought is unclear. However, in this diary entry she focuses on Cohen's emphases on the monotheistic God and juxtaposes this concept of God with her Catholic faith in a Triune God, one God in three persons. On Cohen, see Scott Edgar, "Hermann Cohen," in *The Stanford Encyclopedia of Philosophy* (Winter 2012 ed.), ed. Edward N. Zalta, http:// plato.stanford.edu/ archives/win2012/entries/cohen/.

135. The Sinai Covenant also known as the Mosaic Covenant refers to the covenant between God and Moses on behalf of the Israelite people made on Mount Sinai and realized in the giving and acceptance of divine law. It is described in Exodus 19–24.

136. Salve Regina, or Hail Holy Queen, is a hymn in honor of Mary, the mother of God, sung or recited during Ordinary Time. It is believed to have been composed by Herman Contractus (of Reichenau) in the eleventh century.

Epilogue

BY ERNA BECKER-KOHEN

TWENTY-EIGHT YEARS HAVE PASSED SINCE GUSTAV, MY LIFE partner, died in Bregenz as a consequence of his imprisonment in a concentration camp. He sacrificed himself for me and our son, and it was only because of his sacrifice that we were able to survive.

After a long time, I once again came across these chronicles. As I am examining them anew, I once more ask myself the question that I have so often posed to myself in the past: How did I find my way to the Catholic faith?

I spent my youth, which was already overshadowed by racial hatred, in a Jewish family without ever really getting to know Judaism. Moreover, my parents consciously raised me as a German, We did not see a contradiction between our affiliation with the Jewish religion and our German nationality. Due to my upbringing, the fact that I was a Jew only ever meant to me that I belonged to a different religion than my girlfriends in school. Therefore, I experienced no problems when I later married a Christian man. After all, I had hardly any ties to Judaism in general.

Even though Gustav never attempted to influence me with respect to religion, his exemplary deportment roused my curiosity about his faith. Then, when all values around me became questionable and my uncertainty grew, I continually searched for security. One day, as my fear of what was to come became ever greater, I decided to knock on the doors of the Jesuit College in Berlin to talk with a priest. Father Stromberg listened to me, full of understanding.[1] Following our initial conversation, he agreed to instruct me in the Catholic faith and for a long time I visited the Jesuit residence twice a week. These were hours of feeling safe, but also of internal struggle. How ought I to comprehend that people among whom I lived and who called themselves Christian could be so full of hatred and malice? After all, Christ preached love. But then I met people who lived out their Christian faith. I saw a light and yearned to be one of them, and so, approximately one year later, near the end of 1936, I was baptized.

Afterward I experienced frequent doubts. Was I on the right path? Even though I had had little to do with Judaism, could I turn from it during such difficult times? The faith in the Trinity also posed great difficulties for me. I recalled my childhood when my mother prayed with me in the evening: *Shma Yisrael* (Israel), hear Israel, the eternal God, the one God.[2] That was pretty much all I knew about Judaism. Thus the faith in a Triune God, a God in three persons, struck me as slightly idolatrous. For a long time, I had many debates about it with Catholic priests. But later I grew more settled even on this point. I came to understand that God remains a mystery to us humans, and that we will never be able to comprehend Him with our minds alone. But we can most certainly approach Him through our faith, which has deeper roots in us than our minds. When by chance I went to Grüssau at Easter in 1937 and attended Mass at the Benedictine church,[3] I heard Gregorian chant sung by the monks for the first time in my life.[4] What I heard there manifestly spoke directly to the depth of my soul. I was so moved that for several days, I sat in the church for all the hours of prayer. Now the path to the Catholic faith truly lay open before me.

March 1980

NOTES

1. St. Peter Canisius Preparatory High School (St. Petrus Canisius Kolleg) is a Gymnasium (university preparatory school entailing classical education) in Berlin-Charlottenburg. Father Rudolf Stromberg (1903–1982) was parochial vicar of St. Canisius, the parish adjacent to the St. Peter Canisius Preparatory High School.

2. In the Jewish tradition, the *Shma Yisrael* is said as part of both morning and evening prayers. It is from Deuteronomy 6:4–6:9. Erna recalls saying the prayer at night, referred to as the recitation of the *Shma* in bed. It is the last prayer that a person prays before going to sleep at night, a declaration of faith in the monotheistic God of Israel. Erna's German differs slightly from the Hebrew that is commonly translated in English as "Hear O Israel, the Lord is our God, the Lord is one." The editors wish to thank Shari Lowin for providing this explanation.

3. Erna refers to the former Benedictine Grüssau Abbey located then in Grüssau, Lower Silesia, Germany (now Krzeszów, Poland). Founded in the thirteenth century by Cistercian monks, it was closed under secularization. Following the First World War, German-speaking Benedictine monks expelled from Prague took up residency in the former Cistercian abbey. In 1940, the Gestapo confiscated the abbey, limiting the monks' use of it. Following the Second World War, the region returned to Poland and, in 1946, the Grüssau monks relocated to Bad Wimpfen in Baden-Württemberg. In 2004, due to the dwindling number of monks, those remaining moved to Heidelberg to join with the Benedictines at Neuberg Abbey. See Freunde der Abtei Grüssau, Heimatgeschichte, "Geschichte," http://abtei -gruessau.eu/.

4. Chant used in Catholic liturgies and in the Divine Office (Liturgy of the Hours), which originated during the Medieval Ages, especially under Pope Gregory I "the Great" (590–604).

Afterword

BY ESTHER-MARIA NÄGELE

Only the one who knows the dark,
Who longs for the Light's spark,
Who flees from wickedness
And only sees goodness
Can be certain of victory
And wholly be free.
(From a poem by Erna Becker-Kohen, dedicated to her son, Silvan[1])

More than twenty years have passed since I last held in my hands my grandmother's diary. All the more was my surprise when, so long after its initial publication in German (1980), I received a request from America for an English translation of the diary. As I read my grandmother's work again, I discovered that with the passage of time her words have taken on new meaning and importance.

In today's world, "displacement," "persecution," and "discrimination" have once again become pressing issues. Not since the Second World War have so many people been forced to flee their homelands. Even more troubling is the fact that most of these people did not take flight for economic reasons, but rather because they feared for their lives on account of their political and religious convictions. In Nazi Germany, Jews and opponents of the regime took flight for the same reasons. Under the guise of religion, terrorist organizations such as ISIS, al-Qaeda, the Taliban, and Boko Haram carry out massacres at home and abroad that evoke images of Nazi brutality.

The request by the editors to write an afterword for the English edition of my grandmother's diary forced me once again to face my own painful past. It was only as I wrote these lines that I came to understand how closely my grandmother's story is linked to my own past. Recording her horrific experiences during the Second World War helped my grandmother, at least in part, to come to terms with the past. My father was more reticent. He withdrew and talked little about the war and his years on the run. My father and grandmother also had great difficulties beginning a new life after the war.

After completing his law degree, my father desperately searched for employment in southern Germany. By then, he had to provide for a small family. Unable to find a job, he had to move to nearby Cologne in the Rhineland where he obtained a position with the Bundesamt für Verfassungsschutz, the domestic intelligence service of the Federal Republic of Germany. From there he rose to become a senior government official (*Regierungsdirektor*) responsible for the Middle East. In addition to the extensive responsibilities the position entailed, my father was duty bound to maintain secrecy about his job, a requirement that took a considerable emotional toll on him. He could not talk to anyone about his work, not even his own family. My father was already rather quiet and reserved on account of his experiences during the war, and his work at the domestic intelligence service inevitably made him even more diffident.

He eventually found respite in the Sahara. He loved the isolation and vastness of the landscape. The desert's inhabitants also fascinated him. My mother shared his passion and accompanied him on numerous expeditions. Beginning at the age of four, I was allowed to discover these faraway places with my parents. In March 1994, my parents once again embarked on an expedition to Africa. Their destination was the Libyan Desert. It became a journey of no return. South of the Libyan coastal city of Sirte, strangers robbed and physically assaulted my parents so gravely that both subsequently died. I was unable to accompany them on this trip because, at the time, I was completing my studies in geography at the University of Cologne. I owe my life to this circumstance.

Silvan Becker and Vera Herberg in 1964. Courtesy of Esther-Maria Nägele.

About a month after the brutal attack, I learned from the German embassy of the tragedy that had befallen my parents. By that time, my mother had already died alone without her family in a hospital in Tripoli. I immediately went to see my father, who had been transferred to a military hospital just south of Tripoli. He was in a coma and died two days after my arrival. On the day before his death, he squeezed my hand in farewell. Despite his serious injuries, he had waited for me to arrive so that he could say good-bye to his only daughter.

From one day to the next, nothing was as it had been before. I felt as if the ground was giving way beneath my feet. I loved my parents so very much. We had a special bond. All of a sudden, I was alone, without a family. But just as my grandmother found well-meaning people who supported her during the Second World War, I likewise found such people who supported me. First and foremost, there was my boyfriend, Matthias, now my husband, who accompanied me on the difficult journey to Libya and who did not leave my side, day or night, in the weeks following my parents' deaths. To this day, he continues to be my anchor whenever I descend into the deep and sorrowful valleys of the past. I could also count on my parents' decade-long friendship with a family in southern Germany who took me in and treated me like their own child. In this sheltered and safe environment, I was able to prepare for my final exams. Many years ago, my parents had traveled to the east and because I was too little to come along, I stayed with this family for six weeks. Back then, my mother asked her friend, Ingrid, to take care of me in case something should happen to her and my father. Ingrid kept the promise that she had made to my mother more than twenty years earlier. Her care for me after my parents' deaths was touching.

In retrospect, the many things that befell my grandmother and me in the course of our lives seem less like coincidences than genuine fate. Thus, I am firmly convinced that it was not mere coincidence that I met my husband, Matthias, in 1986, in the middle of the Sahara during a trip to southern Algeria with my parents. Living in different cities, Cologne (Germany) and Feldkirch (Austria), we maintained a long-distance relationship for over eight years. But even through stormy times our love has endured. I also think it a blessing that I am allowed to live in the country where my grandmother and father found shelter among so many courageous and helpful people.

My children attend a school located in direct proximity to the former secondary school, Stella Matutina, that my father attended for a few years after the war. The encounter of my paternal grandmother, Erna Becker-Kohen, with my maternal grandmother, Maria Herberg, in Berlin, is for me seminal. Although denunciations had become routine in Nazi Germany, Erna could trust Maria without hesitation. I feel it was a singular stroke of fate that after countless traumatic events, my parents found each other and fell in love. My mother, Vera, and my grandmother, Maria, too, became refugees when, in 1961, they left their home in East Germany shortly before the construction of the Berlin Wall. Fearing government repression, they fled to West Germany.

It was not until many years later, shortly after the September 11, 2001, terror attacks on the World Trade Center, that I started to doubt that my parents had fallen victim to a robbery. I grew more suspicious that the attack on my parents was politically motivated. Recently, I also learned that one of my parents' assassins most likely participated in the attacks of September 11.

The particular tragedy of my parents' death is that my father miracu-
lously survived the Holocaust only to be murdered by terrorists fifty years
later alongside his wife, on account of his position in the government.

Inevitably, the question as to "why" arises. Why do some people have
to endure such unspeakable suffering, whereas others sail through life
seemingly without any worries? I resisted the term "fate" that was so often
evoked in connection with my parents' murder. Strictly speaking, fate is
an invisible, nameless higher power that guides our lives. It has something of an inevitable ring to it. But most catastrophes on this earth are
human-made and are thus by no means inevitable. Human beings persecuted my grandmother and murdered millions of others during the
Second World War. Years later, human beings took my parents from me
in a most cruel manner. It is telling that my grandmother wrote in her
diary that she feared men more than bombs.

My grandmother found strength in her faith, and her love and respon-
sibility for my father kept her alive. Just like her, I find strength and hope
in my family, in particular in my three children, who show me every day
why life is a gift.

In the end, my parents remained refugees for their entire lives. In particular, my father found security and peace only in the remoteness of the
desert. I, too, am a reserved person, albeit endowed with a somewhat
combative character. I avoid large gatherings and feel most comfortable
in my small circle of friends. I share my parents' love for the Sahara, but
in light of the past tragic events, I will never again set foot in the African
desert. Like my grandmother, I, too, cannot harbor hatred for the people
who have caused me this unspeakable suffering. I will always treasure in
my heart the Sahara Desert's breathtaking landscape, its unforgettable
nomadic inhabitants, and its indescribable atmosphere, which I was allowed to experience with my parents. Even though my parents have been
dead for more than twenty years, I still feel their closeness and protection. Whenever I gaze into the faces of my children, I discover their as-
tonishing similarities to my parents who, I am certain, live on in them.

For me, my grandmother's diary, which is representative of so many
persecuted people during the Second World War, is a memorial entreat-
ing us never to forget the past. It is also an appeal to future generations
to struggle peacefully against dictatorial and totalitarian regimes as well

as crimes against humanity. At the same time, it is a plea that our shared humanity and vulnerable courage will always be a source of hope that will deepen and strengthen our ability to unleash undreamed-of powers of goodness and discovery in our world. More than ever today, every one of us is called upon to contribute to the peaceful coexistence of peoples of different nationalities, confessions, and cultures.

Retrospect

When in the silence of twilight
I examine my life,
I know that it is God's will
That stirs me right.

I once lived in secure tranquility
Without a care, but without God
So that I could do God's will;
But anguish got me instead.

Homeless and without peace,
I wandered aimlessly from place to place.
I soon learned that no safe refuges
Dwell in God's grace.

I often sought to count on people
But never found the right ones.
I placed my trust in them and they misled me
When I weighed my wounds.

The soul is empty, death is near.
I longed only for obliteration, an end,
Or simply salvation from misery
As if it were a friend.

God, you have permitted it.
You even let me sink quite far, adrift;
But then I was able to grasp your hands
And embrace your Love and grip.

Then you let me find
Peace on hallowed ground
So that my soul could find rest
Without discordant sounds.

Lord, I have found you.
Full of gratitude, I examine my life.
My soul was able to heal
In your redemptive light.

I will never again leave you, Lord,
Never again go astray.
Despair will be abhorrent to me
As past delinquent days.
(A poem by Erna Becker-Kohen, dedicated to her son, Silvan[2])

NOTES

1. Poem translated by the editors. The poet James William Chichetto, C.S.C., nuanced the editors' translation into a poetic form.

2. Ibid.

Erna Becker-Kohen (1906–1987), a German Catholic of Jewish heritage, in this memoir recounts her harrowing story of survival on the run in Hitler's Germany.

Martina Cucchiara is Assistant Professor of History at Bluffton University in Ohio.

Esther-Maria Nägele is the granddaughter of Erna Becker-Kohen. She studied geography at the University of Cologne.

Kevin P. Spicer, C.S.C., is James J. Kenneally Distinguished Professor of History at Stonehill College. He is author of *Hitler's Priests: Catholic Clergy and National Socialism* and *Resisting the Third Reich: The Catholic Clergy in Hitler's Berlin,* and editor of *Antisemitism, Christian Ambivalence and the Holocaust* (Indiana University Press).

CPSIA information can be obtained
at www.ICGtesting.com
Printed in the USA
BVHW072158101122
651502BV00025B/420